MW01703329

THE ART OF PATIENT RE-ENGAGEMENT:

HOW TO WIN BACK YOUR **INACTIVE PATIENTS**

CASE STUDY:
How a Dental Office booked
40 appointments each month?

THE ART OF PATIENT RE-ENGAGEMENT:

ABOUT THE **AUTHOR**

Samad Syed is the CEO and Founder of SRS Web Solutions, a Minneapolis, MN-based company that developed the leading dental software platform, mConsent. mConsent is All-in-One Digital Transformation Solution for Dental Offices which helps the front office go paperless, thereby improving Dental office productivity and improving Patient experience. Over 32 million patients across the USA have utilized mConsent software to go paperless, leading to improved patient experience and increased office productivity.

In addition to his work in the dental industry, Samad is a Six Sigma Master Black Belt and has trained over 400 business leaders on bringing productivity and profitability to their businesses using Six Sigma methodology. Samad completed his Master's in Engineering from Wayne State University in Michigan and holds an MBA from Indiana University.

Samad lives in Dallas, TX with his wife Saba and son Yousuf. His educational background and extensive experience in the dental industry have made him a respected and sought-after expert in the field.

Samad's passion for improving patient experience and helping dental practices grow has led him to write "The Art of Patient Re-engagement: How to Win Back Your Inactive Patients". His hope is that the book will help dental practices achieve higher patient retention rates, increase revenue, and provide better patient care.

TABLE OF **CONTENTS**

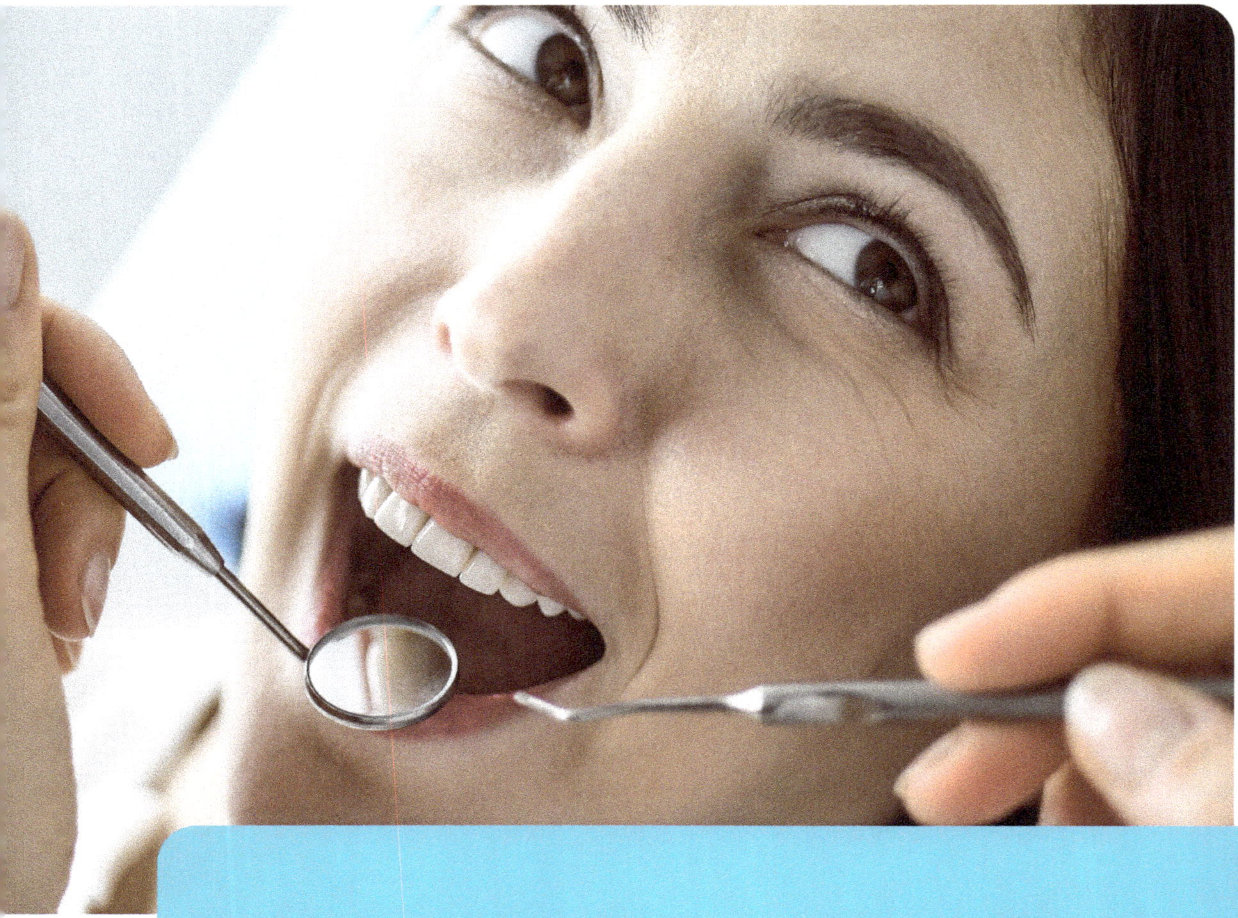

01

INTRODUCTION: UNDERSTANDING THE IMPORTANCE OF PATIENT RE-ENGAGEMENT

DEFINITION OF PATIENT RE-ENGAGEMENT:

Patient re-engagement refers to the approach of reaching out to patients who have not received dental care for a specific period and inviting them to return to the practice. This approach aims to establish and sustain relationships with patients who may have stopped visiting the dental practice for reasons such as schedule conflicts, financial constraints, or change of healthcare providers. The main objective of patient re-engagement is to build patient loyalty, enhance their health outcomes, and increase the practice's revenue. Achieving this requires utilizing personalized follow-up, reminders and notifications, direct mail, and improving the overall patient experience. By using these techniques, dental practices can restore connections with patients who have been inactive, address their needs and concerns, and encourage them to return for dental care.

> **"The key to a thriving dental practice is not just attracting new patients, but also keeping existing patients engaged and active. Identifying and analyzing inactive patients is the first step towards re-engaging them and ensuring the long-term success of your practice."**

WHY RE-ENGAGING INACTIVE PATIENTS IS CRITICAL FOR DENTAL PRACTICES

Re-engaging inactive patients is critical for dental practices for several reasons

1. **Increases patient loyalty:** Re-engaging inactive patients can help to establish a strong, long-term relationship between the practice and the patient. The practice will have a steady patient base as a result of greater patient retention. Also, this strategy may encourage patient loyalty, which will help the practice succeed as a whole.

2. **Improves health outcomes:** Dental offices that contact people who haven't been in for a long can improve their general health. This is so that patients can experience better health outcomes as a result of early diagnosis, treatments, and preventative care made possible by routine dental care. Dental offices may significantly improve their patients' health by encouraging patient retention and offering regular care.

3. **Increases revenue:** Dental practices may benefit financially from reaching out to inactive patients. Practices can increase their revenue and attain better financial stability by offering them appointments that would otherwise go vacant. By using this strategy, practices can maximize their use of their financial performance and resource availability.

4. **Supports practice growth:** Dental practices must put a strong emphasis on re-engaging inactive patients if they want to expand and grow. This entails keeping current patients while luring new ones, which can aid in the growth and success of practices. Practices can achieve sustainable development and ongoing success by focusing on patient retention and outreach.

5. **Helps to build brand reputation:** By providing outstanding patient care and involvement, dental practices can establish a great reputation in their neighborhood. New patients may be drawn in as a result, and the practice's general reputation may be improved. Dental practices can position themselves as reputable and trustworthy healthcare organization in their community by putting a priority on patient happiness and concentrating on developing close relationships with patients. In the end, this might result in the practice's continued success and expansion.

CASE STUDY:

Crescent Family Dental is a bustling dental office located in a suburban area of Chicago. With several years of operation under their belt, the practice had established a loyal patient base. However, over time, many of these patients began to fall inactive. The practice had been so focused on attracting new patients that they had overlooked the importance of engaging with their existing ones.

Recognizing the significance of re-engaging inactive patients, the management team at Crescent Family Dental took action. They initiated a targeted outreach campaign to re-engage these patients and motivate them to return to the practice. This was a crucial step towards ensuring the continued success and growth of the practice.

The dental practice started by conducting a thorough analysis of patient records to determine which patients had become inactive. Using this information, they created a list of these patients and then organized them into specific groups based on their treatment history and previous behavior.

After segmenting the inactive patients, the dental practice then began a targeted outreach campaign. They utilized personalized follow-up messages that emphasized the importance of routine dental care and provided incentives for returning patients. Additionally, they set up a reminder system that included text and email alerts to keep patients up-to-date on upcoming appointments.

To improve the overall patient experience, the practice invested in new technology that included online booking and appointment reminders. They also made changes to the physical office environment and provided additional staff training to ensure a welcoming and friendly experience for all patients.

Crescent Family Dental monitored their development throughout the first 3 months to evaluate the success of their re-engagement effort. They were happy to learn that, after 6 months, they had effectively reactivated more than 10% of their inactive patients. Due to their efforts, the practice saw an increase in revenue and patient loyalty.

The management team at CFD learned from this experience how crucial it is to put existing patients first in order to preserve a profitable and long-lasting dental office. They were able to build a solid reputation in their community and draw in new patients by putting a strong emphasis on offering outstanding patient care and involvement, which contributed to their overall success.

To sum up, this case study highlights the importance of re-engaging inactive patients for dental practices to achieve long-term success.

By implementing patient re-engagement strategies and prioritizing the patient experience, dental practices can not only improve patient health outcomes, but also increase revenue and foster growth and success of the practice.

PATIENT RE-ENGAGEMENT VS MARKETING FOR NEW PATIENTS

Dental practices must consider the advantages and disadvantages of each strategy when deciding between patient re-engagement and patient-attraction marketing. Re-engaging with inactive patients can significantly affect patient loyalty and retention rates, while bringing in new patients can broaden a practice's clientele. In the end, the decision between the two approaches will be based on the particular requirements and objectives of the practice.

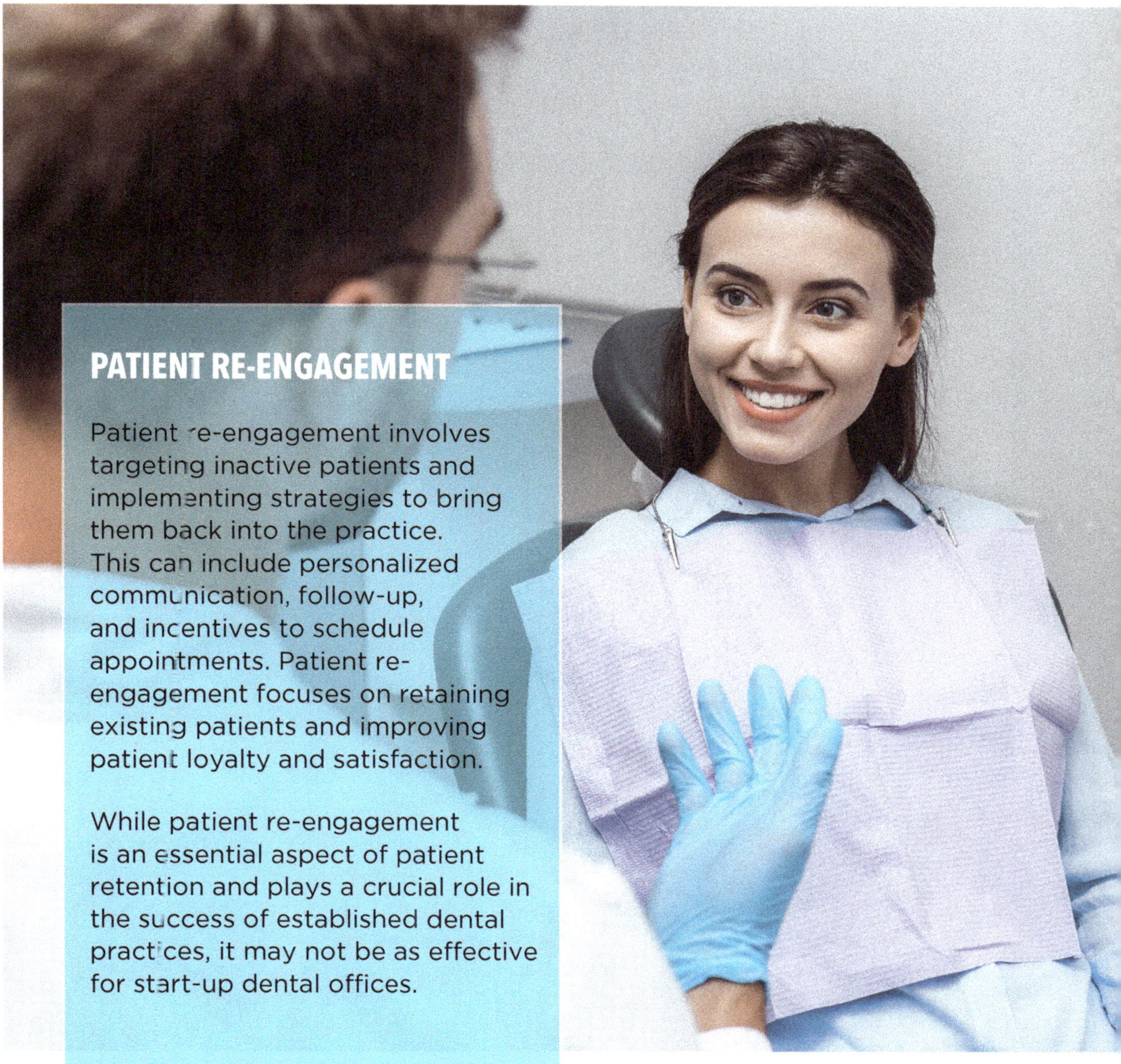

PATIENT RE-ENGAGEMENT

Patient re-engagement involves targeting inactive patients and implementing strategies to bring them back into the practice. This can include personalized communication, follow-up, and incentives to schedule appointments. Patient re-engagement focuses on retaining existing patients and improving patient loyalty and satisfaction.

While patient re-engagement is an essential aspect of patient retention and plays a crucial role in the success of established dental practices, it may not be as effective for start-up dental offices.

BENEFITS OF PATIENT RE-ENGAGEMENT:

1. **Cost-effective:** Typically, re-engaging inactive patients is a more cost-effective approach than marketing to attract new patients. The cost of acquiring a new patient can be up to five times higher than retaining an existing patient.

2. **Increased patient loyalty:** By re-engaging inactive patients, dental practices can foster greater patient loyalty and satisfaction. Patients who are re-engaged are more likely to continue receiving care from the dental practice, refer others to the practice, and leave positive reviews. This can help to establish a strong reputation for the practice and promote future growth and success.

3. **Improved patient outcomes:** When dental practices re-engage with inactive patients, they have an opportunity to provide tailored care and follow-up to at-risk patients, leading to improved patient outcomes. By identifying potential oral health issues early and providing targeted communication, dental practices can prevent further complications and promote positive patient outcomes.

4. **Stronger patient relationships:** Patient engagement and satisfaction can increase when patients feel valued and connected to their dental office through personalized communication, follow-up, and treatment.

5. **Increased revenue:** Active patients are more likely to schedule appointments, accept treatment plans, and recommend the practice to others, leading to greater revenue over time.

MARKETING FOR NEW PATIENTS

Marketing techniques including advertising, direct mail, social media marketing, and search engine optimization are needed to draw new patients to a dental office. Expanding the patient base and generating more new business are the main objectives of marketing to new patients.

BENEFITS OF MARKETING FOR NEW PATIENTS:

1. **Increased patient volume:** Marketing for new patients can attract a large volume of new patients to the practice, leading to a potential increase in revenue.

2. **Potential for growth:** Marketing for new patients can help dental practices expand their patient base and grow their business.

3. **Improved visibility:** Implementing marketing strategies to attract new patients can help dental practices increase their visibility and establish their position as a reputable and high-quality dental care provider in the community.

4. **Access to new markets:** Marketing for new patients can help dental practices reach new markets and demographics.

5. **Brand building:** Marketing for new patients can help to establish the practice's brand and reputation.

COMPARISON OF PATIENT RE-ENGAGEMENT VS MARKETING FOR NEW PATIENTS:

Getting new patients and re-engaging with former patients are the two main marketing tactics for expanding a dental practice. Using data analysis from a dental general practice, we will compare the efficiency of these two methodologies in this chapter.

The practice heavily invested in new patient marketing from February 2022 to April 2022, using various channels like Google ads, Facebook ads, SEO, direct mail, and marketing agencies. The targeted population was within a 5-mile radius, and the age group was 19 and above.

New Patient Marketing Campaign	Cost Incurred for 3 months	ReEngagement Campaign	Cost Incurred for 3 months
Target Population - 5 miles (Age:19+)		Target Population	~2500 inactive patients (>1year)
Google Ads	$3000	Google Ads + Facebook Remarketing	$750
Facebook Ads	$3000	SMS + Email Campaign	$400
SEO	$1500	Direct Mail Ads	$3500
Direct Mail Ads	$3500	Website+Landing Pages	$1000
Marketing Agency	$2800	Digital tools+Marketing Agency cost	$2200
Total Cost	$13,800	**Total Cost**	$7850
Cost of New Pat. Acq	$260	**Cost of Appt completed:**	$70
RESULTS Appointments booked: 76 Appointment Completed: 53	Est. Revenue: $500 x 53 **$26,500**	Appointments booked: 148 Appointment Completed: 112	Est. Revenue: $500 x 112 **$56,000**

This analysis demonstrates the potential cost savings and revenue benefits of patient re-engagement in comparison to new patient acquisition. Re-engaging inactive patients is more cost-effective as they are already familiar with the practice and its services, increasing the likelihood of them returning for future visits. Furthermore, re-engaging patients can lead to higher revenue potential as they are more likely to accept treatment plans.

In this case study, re-engaging 112 inactive patients cost $7,850, while acquiring 53 new patients cost $13,800. The estimated revenue generated from new patient acquisition was $26,500, whereas the estimated revenue generated from patient re-engagement was $56,000. These results demonstrate the potential for a higher return on investment with patient re-engagement strategies.

In the dental industry, it's crucial for practices to weigh the pros and cons of investing in patient re-engagement versus marketing for new patients. In general, patient re-engagement can offer more cost savings and long-term benefits compared to new patient acquisition campaigns.

By prioritizing patient re-engagement strategies, practices can retain existing patients, build patient loyalty, and improve patient outcomes. On the other hand, marketing for new patients tends to focus on expanding the patient base and attracting new business, which can be more expensive and may not result in long-term patient retention or loyalty. It's important for practices to consider their goals and budget when deciding which approach to take.

UNDERSTANDING THE CHALLENGES OF RE-ENGAGING INACTIVE PATIENTS

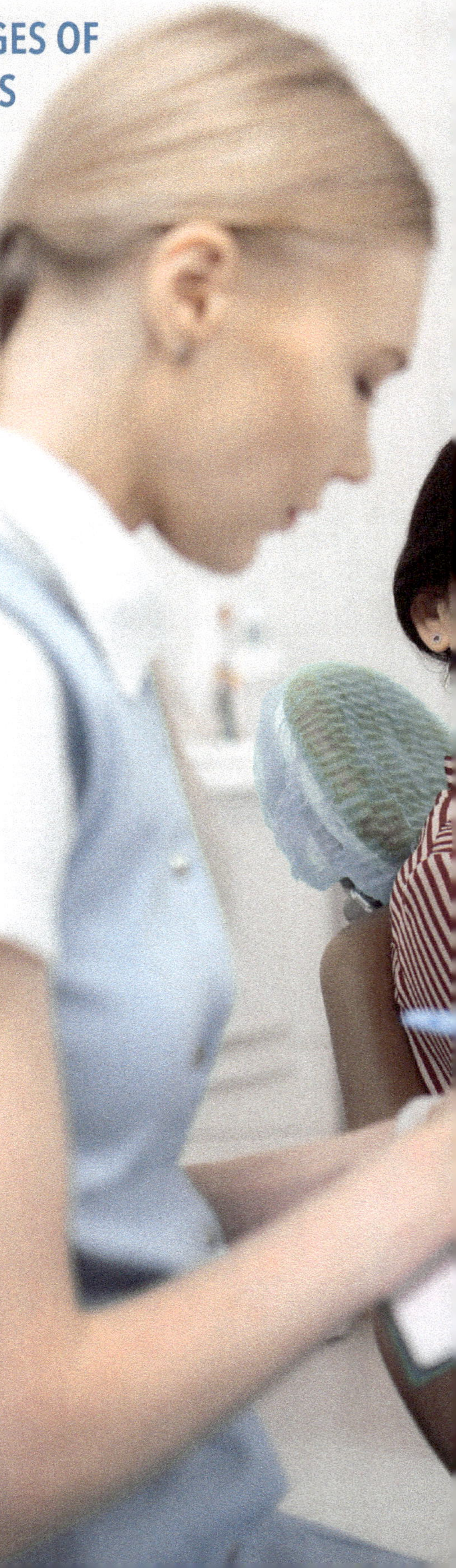

Re-engaging inactive patients can be a challenge for dental practices, as patients often have many reasons for not coming back to the office. Some of the challenges of re-engaging inactive patients include:

1. **Competition:**
   There are many dental practices in the market, and inactive patients may have switched to a different practice.

2. **Cost:**
   Dental treatments can be expensive, and inactive patients may have decided to forgo treatment due to financial reasons.

3. **Lack of Awareness:**
   Inactive patients may not be aware of the importance of regular dental care, and may not see the value in coming back to the office.

4. **Negative Experience:**
   Some inactive patients may have had a negative experience at the practice, such as long wait times or poor customer service, and may not want to return.

5. **Busy Schedules:**
   Patients may have busy schedules and find it difficult to make time for dental appointments.

6. **Fear of Dental Procedures:**
   Re-engaging inactive patients can be hindered by dental anxiety or fear, which can prevent patients from returning to the office.

Re-engaging inactive patients can be a significant challenge for dental practices, as patients have various reasons for not coming back to the office. One of the most critical internal factors is finding the right tools to re-engage patients. Mass text messaging, emails, and building the right flow to get inactive patients to set up an appointment can be a challenging task. Dental practices may also face challenges with staff trying to handle the re-engagement process themselves, leading to inadequate results.

ABC Dental (name changed for privacy), a small dental practice, was facing a challenge of declining patient numbers. Over the years, they had lost touch with many of their inactive patients and had a difficult time getting them to come back for appointments. This was impacting their bottom line and they needed to find a solution to re-engage these inactive patients.

Dental team conducted a study to explore the reasons for patient inactivity by making 50 calls to inactive patients. The findings revealed that many patients had switched to another dental practice, faced financial constraints, or had forgotten about their appointments, thus shedding light on the reasons behind patient inactivity.

With this quick phone survey, they found out what's causing the decline in patient re-engagement. It allowed the practice to see the gaps and build a strategy for re-engaging the patients.

COST OF IGNORING PATIENT RE-ENGAGEMENT:

Dental practices use patient re-engagement as a key approach to boost revenue, retain more patients, and deliver better results for oral health. But neglecting patient re-engagement can cost dental practices a lot of money. In this section, we'll look at the costs associated with neglecting patient re-engagement in dentistry and explain why dental practices should make it a top priority.

COSTS OF IGNORING PATIENT RE-ENGAGEMENT IN DENTISTRY:

1. **Decreased Patient Retention:** Dental practices that neglect patient re-engagement may have lower patient retention, which may lead patients to seek care elsewhere and lower revenue. In addition, patients who feel forgotten or ignored can write bad reviews or tell others about their experiences, which would be detrimental to the practice's reputation.

2. **Missed Opportunities for Treatment:** Patients who have disengaged from the dental practice may have oral health issues that need to be addressed. Ignoring patient re-engagement can lead to missed opportunities for treatment and may result in more serious and costly procedures down the line. This can also result in a loss of revenue for the practice.

3. **Increased Costs:** Dentists may incur higher expenditures if they ignore patient re-engagement. This is due to the fact that maintaining current patients can often be more expensive than acquiring new ones. Also, former patients can have more serious oral health problems that call for more expensive operations.

4. **Reduced Revenue:** When patients become disengaged from a dental practice, they may choose to receive care from another provider, resulting in a loss of revenue for the practice. This can be particularly detrimental if the patient has undergone high-value procedures or treatments in the past.

5. **Reduced Quality of Care:** Failure to prioritize patient re-engagement can result in a decline in the quality of care that patients receive. Neglected patients may not receive the necessary treatments and preventative care required to maintain good oral health, which can lead to more severe health issues in the future.

CONCLUSION:

To sum up, dental practices that neglect patient re-engagement can face various costs, including negative impact on patient outcomes and loss of revenue. By prioritizing patient re-engagement, dental practices can improve patient retention, increase revenue, and provide better oral health outcomes for their patients.

RECALL VS RE-ENGAGEMENT: WHAT'S THE DIFFERENCE BETWEEN THEM?

INTRODUCTION:

Dental practices use patient recall and patient re-engagement as two key ways to enhance patient outcomes and boost earnings. The distinctions between patient recall and patient re-engagement in dentistry, as well as the advantages of each method, will be covered in this chapter.

PATIENT RECALL:

Patient recall in dentistry refers to the process of reaching out to patients who are due for regular checkups and cleanings every six months. Dental offices typically use email, phone calls, or text reminders to remind patients to schedule an appointment. The goal of patient recall in dentistry is to prevent oral health issues and catch any problems early on, which can lead to better patient outcomes and satisfaction.

There are several benefits to using patient recall in dentistry, including:

1. **Improved Oral Health:** Patient recall in dentistry can help improve oral health outcomes by ensuring that patients receive regular checkups and cleanings.
2. **Increased Revenue:** Patient recall in dentistry can help increase revenue for dental practices by filling empty appointment slots and reducing the need for costly procedures down the line.
3. **Better Patient Engagement:** In dentistry, patient recall is a powerful tool for boosting participation and showing patients that the office cares about their oral health. It helps to make sure that patients get the attention they require to maintain good oral health and avoid the emergence of more significant problems.

PATIENT RE-ENGAGEMENT IN DENTISTRY:

Patient re-engagement in dentistry refers to the process of engaging with patients who have disengaged from the dental practice entirely. This can happen for a variety of reasons, such as moving to a new area, changing insurance providers, or simply forgetting to schedule follow-up appointments.

There are several benefits to using patient re-engagement in dentistry, including:

1. **Improved Patient Retention:** Patient re-engagement in dentistry can help improve patient retention by reconnecting with patients and encouraging them to resume their care.
2. **Increased Revenue:** Patient re-engagement in dentistry can help increase revenue for dental practices by bringing back patients who may have sought care elsewhere.
3. **Better Patient Engagement:** Patient re-engagement in dentistry can help improve patient engagement by showing patients that their dental practice cares about their oral health and wants to ensure they receive the care they need.

WHEN TO USE PATIENT RECALL VS PATIENT RE-ENGAGEMENT IN DENTISTRY:

Determining whether to use patient recall or patient re-engagement in dentistry depends on several factors, including the duration since the patient's last visit, the reason for their inactivity, and their overall oral health status.

Patient recall is usually more appropriate for patients due for regular checkups and cleanings. Patient re-engagement is generally more suitable for patients who have been inactive for a longer period, such as 12 months or more, and may need a more personalized approach.

CONCLUSION:

Patient recall and patient re-engagement are essential components of dental practice management that can help achieve better patient outcomes and revenue growth. By recognizing the differences between these two strategies and determining the appropriate time to use them, dental practices can enhance patient engagement, retention, and overall oral health.

02

UNDERSTANDING **PATIENT BEHAVIOR**

- Reasons why patients become inactive
- Identifying at-risk patients
- The psychology of patient behavior

Effective patient re-engagement requires understanding patient behavior. Patients become inactive for various reasons, and identifying the underlying causes of patient inactivity is crucial to developing effective re-engagement strategies. This chapter discusses the reasons why patients become inactive, identifying at-risk patients, and the psychology of patient behavior.

REASONS WHY PATIENTS BECOME INACTIVE:

The following are the most common reasons why patients become inactive:

1. **Lack of Communication:** When patients feel ignored or overlooked by their dental practice, they are more likely to disengage from the practice. Poor communication or a lack of follow-up from the dental practice can leave patients feeling undervalued or neglected, which can ultimately lead to patient inactivity.

2. **Fear or Anxiety:** Patients who have dental anxiety or fear may avoid dental appointments, leading to inactivity. Dental practices must recognize and address patients' fears and anxieties to encourage them to schedule appointments and engage with the practice.

3. **Cost or Insurance Coverage:** Patients who have limited financial resources or inadequate insurance coverage may avoid dental appointments, leading to inactivity. Dental practices must provide affordable and flexible payment options to encourage patients to schedule appointments and engage with the practice.

4. **Time Constraints:** Patients who have busy schedules or demanding jobs may struggle to find time for dental appointments, leading to inactivity. Dental practices must offer flexible scheduling options, including evening and weekend appointments, to accommodate patients' schedules.

IDENTIFYING AT-RISK PATIENTS:

It is critical to identify patients who are at risk of becoming inactive in order to establish successful re-engagement initiatives. Some signs of a high-risk patient include:

1. **Inactivity:** One of the key markers of at-risk patients is inactivity. Patients who do not make or miss scheduled appointments are more prone to become inactive. Patients may have simply forgotten to book an appointment or had scheduling issues in some circumstances, but in others, inactivity may be due to a lack of perceived value or interest in continuing care with the practice.

2. **Lack of Engagement:** Patients who do not respond to dental practice communication or follow-up are deemed at risk of becoming inactive. This could be due to a variety of factors, including a lack of feeling appreciated, an unpleasant experience with the practice, or a lack of desire in continuing care. It is critical for dental practices to identify and reach out to these individuals in order to keep them active.

3. **Negative Feedback:** Patients who leave negative feedback or reviews may be dissatisfied with their experience, leading to disengagement and possible inactivity. It is important for dental practices to monitor and respond to negative feedback or reviews promptly and address any concerns or complaints to prevent further disengagement.

4. **Health Status:** Patients who have chronic health conditions or who are at risk of developing oral diseases may be more likely to become inactive if they do not feel their care needs are being met. Dental practices must prioritize the care of these patients and communicate the importance of continued care.

THE PSYCHOLOGY OF PATIENT BEHAVIOR:

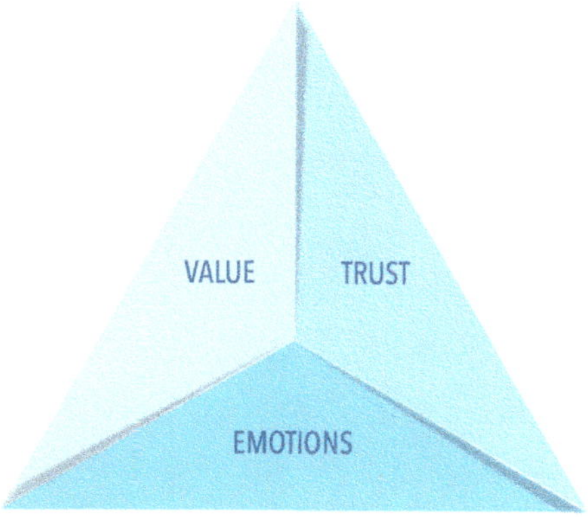

VET MODEL

Understanding the psychology of patient behavior is crucial to developing effective re-engagement strategies. Patients' decisions to engage or disengage with their dental practice are influenced by the VET Model of psychology.

1 Value: **Patients expect to receive value from their dental practice, including personalized care, convenience, and affordability. Dental practices must deliver value to patients to encourage patient engagement, improve patient outcomes, and grow their business.**

Providing patients with high-quality, personalized care that is convenient and affordable is crucial for establishing strong patient relationships and growing a successful dental practice.

Offering tailored treatment programmes is one way dental businesses can add value. This may entail adapting treatment choices to each patient's unique needs and preferences. Dental practices can increase patient results and satisfaction by providing personalized care.

Offering accessible features like flexible scheduling, online appointment booking, and video consultations can help dental businesses increase patient engagement. By giving such options, patients might have easier access to dental treatment and feel more driven to book and attend frequent appointments.

Providing affordable dental care is crucial for delivering value to patients. Dental practices can offer various payment options such as financing and insurance billing to make dental services more accessible and affordable. Clear and upfront pricing information can also help patients make informed decisions about their care, improving patient satisfaction and trust in the practice.

Offering accessible features like flexible scheduling, online appointment booking, and video consultations can help dental businesses increase patient engagement. By giving such options, patients might have easier access to dental treatment and feel more driven to book and attend frequent appointments.

2 Understanding Patient Emotions: Patient emotions significantly influence multiple aspects of their experience in dental care, such as decision-making, adherence to treatment, and overall satisfaction. Dentists need to be aware of patients' emotions to deliver care that meets both their physical and emotional needs. Patients' emotions in dental settings can be categorized into positive and negative emotions:

Positive Emotions:
1. Gratitude
2. Relief
3. Satisfaction

Negative Emotions:
1. Anxiety
2. Fear
3. Frustration

Managing Emotions in Dentistry: To recognize and address patients' emotions, dentists should adopt a proactive approach, ensuring that patients feel supported and understood, ultimately fostering a positive patient experience.

Positive Emotions: Positive emotions help strengthen the bond between patients and dentists, resulting in improved patient satisfaction and adherence to treatment plans. Dentists can enhance positive emotions such as gratitude, relief, and satisfaction by offering high-quality, patient-centered care, following up with patients, establishing rapport, and demonstrating genuine concern for patients' well-being.

Negative Emotions: Negative emotions, including anxiety, fear, and frustration, can hinder the patient-dentist relationship, leading to the avoidance of dental care or decreased satisfaction. Dentists can address these negative emotions by creating a calming atmosphere, thoroughly explaining procedures, offering distractions, providing sedation dentistry options for anxious patients, promoting open communication, employing minimally invasive methods when feasible, using topical anesthetics or numbing agents, optimizing scheduling processes, offering flexible payment options, addressing concerns promptly, and keeping patients updated on treatment progress.

By acknowledging and addressing both positive and negative emotions throughout patients' dental care journey, dentists create a supportive and positive environment that contributes to enhanced patient satisfaction, adherence to treatment, and overall better outcomes. Identifying and managing emotions is an essential aspect of patient-focused care and should be incorporated into dental professionals' daily routines to ensure a comprehensive approach to patient well-being.

3 Trust: Patients must trust their dental practice to provide high-quality care and prioritize their interests. Building patient trust takes time, and dental practices must consistently demonstrate their commitment to patient care.

Building trust is essential for dental practices to succeed. Patients who trust their dental professionals are more likely to return for future visits, refer others to the practice, and comply with recommended treatment plans.

One method to create trust is to communicate clearly about the expense of treatment. Dental professionals should take the time to discuss patient and insurance responsibilities for the cost of treatment, including any out-of-pocket payments. Dental practices may create confidence and avoid surprises or misunderstandings by being clear and upfront about charges.

Developing patient trust is critical to retaining patient involvement in dental clinics. One effective strategy to create trust is to ensure transparent disclosure regarding treatment costs. Dental professionals should communicate to patients and their insurance providers their financial responsibilities for treatment costs, including any out-of-pocket charges. Dental practices may develop confidence and avoid surprises or misconceptions that could lead to patient disengagement by being clear and forthright about expenses.

Prioritizing patient care and safety is also essential for fostering trust. Dental practices should follow tight infection control standards, offer complete dental care, and stay current on new technology and techniques. Dental clinics can establish patient confidence and loyalty by displaying a dedication to patient safety and quality care.

Excellent customer service is also essential for establishing trust. Dental practices should be sensitive to patient needs, provide flexible scheduling alternatives, and handle any problems or issues that occur as soon as possible. Dental practices can build trust and long-term patient relationships by displaying a dedication to patient satisfaction.

Dental practices can create trust with their patients by constantly displaying a dedication to patient care, safety, and satisfaction. This leads to higher patient engagement and retention.

CONCLUSION:

Understanding patient behavior is critical to developing effective patient re-engagement strategies. Patients become inactive for various reasons, including a lack of communication, fear or anxiety, cost or insurance coverage, and time constraints. Identifying at-risk patients and understanding the psychology of patient behavior are essential to developing effective re-engagement strategies. By addressing patients' emotions, building patient trust, and delivering value, dental practices can encourage patient engagement, improve patient outcomes, and grow their business.

03

IDENTIFYING AND ANALYZING **INACTIVE PATIENTS**

“

Re-engaging inactive patients is not just about filling appointment slots, it's about restoring connections, building trust, and ensuring the long-term health and success of your dental practice.

Keeping your patient base engaged and active is crucial to the success of your dental practice. However, for a variety of reasons, patients may become inactive and cease attending your practice. Inactive patients can have a substantial influence on your practice's bottom line, whether it's due to a change in insurance, a move to a new location, or simple forgetfulness.

It is critical for dental practices to have a process in place to identify and assess inactive patients before taking actions to re-engage them. This chapter will look at the hurdles that dental offices experience when re-engaging inactive patients and suggest practical methods to overcome them.

We'll start by defining inactive patients and the impact they can have on your practice. After that, we'll go over the numerous tactics and approaches for identifying and assessing inactive patients, such as demographic analysis, appointment history, and patient surveys.

Following that, we'll go over the various channels dental clinics can utilize to re-engage inactive patients, such as targeted follow-up, reminders and notifications, and patient incentives. We'll also talk about how important it is to have a personalized approach to re-engagement and how technology may help with that.

By the end of this book, you will have a good knowledge of the importance of re-engaging inactive patients as well as effective ways for doing so. Whether you're an experienced dentist or a newcomer, this book will provide you with the tools and knowledge you need to successfully re-engage your inactive patients and enhance the health and prosperity of your business.

WITH 5 SIMPLE STEPS IDENTIFY AND ANALYZE INACTIVE PATIENTS

STEP 1

DEFINE INACTIVITY CRITERIA

To identify and analyze inactive patients, the first step is to define what defines inactivity. These will vary according on your practice, however some common requirements include:

- Patients who have not been seen in over 12 months
- Patients who have missed two or more scheduled appointments in a row
- Patients who have not responded to recent marketing or outreach efforts

STEP 2

REVIEW PATIENT DATA

After you've created your inactivity criterion, go over your patient data. This could include appointment history, demographic data, and records of recent correspondence. This data will assist you in compiling a thorough list of inactive patients and gaining insights into the reasons for their inactivity.

STEP 3

CONDUCT SURVEYS

Another useful method for gathering information on inactive patients and the causes for their inactivity is to conduct surveys. Inactive patients might be contacted via email, phone, or mail and asked a series of questions. This data can be utilized to discover common themes and pain points that can be addressed in future re-engagement initiatives.

STEP 4

SEGMENT INACTIVE PATIENTS

It's important to segment inactive patients into different groups based on their specific characteristics, such as the length of their inactivity, their age, location, or previous treatment history. This will allow you to tailor your re-engagement efforts and create a more personalized approach.

STEP 5

ANALYZE RESULTS

The final step is to assess the outcomes of your efforts to identify inactive patients and collect information about the reasons for their inactivity. This data can help you make informed decisions regarding your re-engagement strategy, such as which channels to employ, what messages to send, and what incentives to offer. The findings of your analysis will also assist you in determining the effectiveness of your re-engagement activities and making any necessary changes moving forward.

How to analyze Inactive patients in your EMR system? This could differ a little based on what EMR you are using (Eaglesoft, Open dental, Dentrix, Curve or Dolphin)

HERE ARE 5 STEPS TO ANALYZE INACTIVE PATIENTS IN YOUR EMR SYSTEM:

1. **Identify Inactivity Criteria:** As described in the previous answer, you should first identify what constitutes inactivity in your practice, 12 months. This information can be used to create a list of inactive patients within your EMR system.

2. **Run Reports:** Utilize your EMR system's reporting features to extract essential patient data, such as appointment history, demographic information, and recent communication records. You can use this data to compile a thorough list of inactive patients and categorize them based on their unique traits.

3. **Analyze Appointment History:** Assess inactive patients' appointment history to find any trends or patterns in their behavior. This could include the number of appointments they had, the type of therapies they received, and the time between appointments.

4. **Evaluate Communication Efforts:** Review the communication records within your EMR system to see if any inactive patients have responded to recent marketing or outreach efforts. This information can be used to identify the most effective communication channels and strategies for re-engaging inactive patients.

5. **Use Data Analytics Tools:** Your EMR system may also have data analytics tools that can be used to analyze inactive patients. These tools can help you identify trends, create predictive models, and make informed decisions about your re engagement strategy.

Background: ABC Dentistry (name changed for privacy) is a modest dental office in the middle of Dallas. The practice has been in operation for over ten years and has a large number of satisfied patients. Yet, the clinic has seen a fall in patient engagement in recent years, with many inactive patients not arranging appointments for more than a year.

Problem: The practice wanted to understand why patients were becoming inactive and how they could re-engage them. The practice decided to analyze patient data and metrics in its EMR system to gain insights into patient behavior.

Steps taken: The practice followed these 5 steps to understand patient data and metrics in the EMR system:

1. **Define Data Requirements:** The practice identified the specific data points it needed to understand inactive patients, including demographics, appointment history, treatment history, and recent communication records.

2. **Retrieve Data:** Utilizing the EMR system's reporting capabilities, the practice gathered important patient data for inactive patients during the previous 12 months. To automate the procedure, the firm also employed a data extraction programme.

3. **Clean and Organize Data:** The procedure ensured that the data was clean and well-organized, allowing for successful analysis. Duplicates were removed, errors were fixed, and data fields were standardized.

4. **Analyze Data:** The practice analyzed the data and generated metrics using data analytics tools. To better understand patient behavior and detect trends and patterns, charts, graphs, and other visual zations were constructed.

5. **Interpret Results:** Upon analyzing the data, the practice discovered that the highest percentage of inactive patients fell within the age range of 25 to 35 years old and had visited the practice only once or twice in the last year. Further analysis showed that these patients had not responded to recent communications, such as appointment reminders and follow-up messages.

Outcome: By analyzing patient data, the dental practice gained valuable insights into patient behavior and preferences. Based on the findings, the practice developed a targeted strategy to re-engage inactive patients, focusing on young adults and utilizing personalized and timely communication methods, such as email and text messaging.

CONCLUSION

By understanding patient data and metrics in the EMR system, ABC Dental was able to gain valuable insights into patient behavior and develop a targeted re-engagement strategy that helped win back inactive patients and improve the overall health of the practice.

04

DEVELOPING A **RE-ENGAGEMENT** STRATEGY

This chapter aims to provide guidance on developing a patient re-engagement strategy that is customized to your dental practice's specific requirements. By following the steps outlined, from identifying your target audience to setting realistic goals, you will be able to develop a strategy that meets your objectives. Whether you're a seasoned professional or new to the industry, this chapter is an invaluable resource for successfully re-engaging inactive patients.

SETTING OBJECTIVES AND GOALS:

"Establishing specific and attainable objectives and targets is critical for any effective patient re-engagement approach. It is impossible to measure the impact of your efforts and establish which techniques are working and which need to be improved without a well-defined plan. Let's look at the most important aspects of developing objectives and goals for your patient re-engagement strategy. We will walk you through the processes to establish a focused, effective, and results-driven strategy, from identifying metrics to track progress to setting specific, quantifiable targets. Whether you're a seasoned pro or just getting started, this chapter is a must-read for developing a successful patient re-engagement plan.."

FEW STEPS TO STEPS TO START WITH OBJECTIVES AND GOALS:

1 **Assess the Current Situation:** The first step in developing an effective patient re-engagement strategy is to assess the current situation. This involves identifying the number of inactive patients, determining the reasons for their inactivity, and evaluating the practice's current patient engagement practices.

2 **Define Objectives:** Once the current situation is understood, it's time to set objectives and goals for the patient re-engagement strategy. Objectives should be specific, measurable, attainable, relevant, and time-bound (SMART). For example, the goal could be to increase the number of active patients by 20% in the next six months.

3 **Example of a Good Objective:** "To re-engage 150 inactive patients in the next quarter, who have not visited our practice in over 12 months, by offering a 10% discount on their next appointment for preventive care."

4 **Example of a Bad Objective:** "To get more patients to come back to our practice."

5 **Identify Target Audience:** Identifying the target audience is crucial in developing an effective re-engagement strategy. For example, the practice may target patients who have not visited the practice in the past 12 months, those who have not had a regular cleaning in the past 24 months, or those who have not had any treatments in the past 36 months.

6 **Example of a Good Target Audience:** "Inactive female cosmetic patients between the ages of 25-35, who have not visited our practice in the last 18 months, and have previously received preventive care."

7 **Example of a Bad Target Audience:** "All inactive patients."

8 **Choose Re-engagement Channels:** Based on the target audience and objectives, practices can choose the most effective re-engagement channels. This can include direct mail, email, text message reminders, social media, and patient portals, among others.

9 **Develop a Re-engagement Plan:** Once objectives and channels are identified, the next step is to develop a re-engagement plan. This plan should include specific actions, deadlines, and milestones, and should be reviewed and updated regularly.

10 **Evaluate and Refine:** The final step is to evaluate and refine the patient re-engagement strategy. This involves monitoring progress, tracking results, and making adjustments as needed. By regularly reviewing and refining the strategy, practices can continuously improve patient engagement and achieve their re-engagement objectives.

In summary, developing an effective patient re-engagement strategy at a dental practice involves assessing the current situation, defining objectives and goals, identifying the target audience, choosing re-engagement channels, developing a re-engagement plan, and evaluating and refining the strategy regularly.

UNDERSTANDING THE PATIENT JOURNEY:

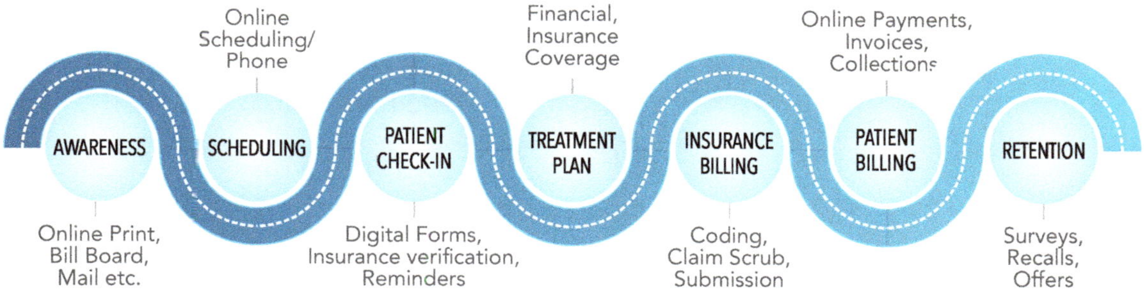

The patient journey is an essential component of any successful patient re-engagement strategy. It provides valuable insights into how patients interact with your dental practice and what motivates them to return for appointments. Understanding the patient journey can help you identify opportunities to improve the patient experience, increase patient engagement, and drive results.

To increase the chances of a patient returning to your dental clinic, it's important to analyze their entire experience and identify areas where improvements can be made. By mapping out every touchpoint and interaction a patient has with your practice, you can better understand their journey and develop a strategy that targets their needs. In this chapter, we will guide you through the process of analyzing the patient experience and using that knowledge to create a focused and effective patient re-engagement plan.

Step 1 Map out the patient journey. This involves identifying all of the different interactions and touchpoints a patient has with your dental practice, from their initial contact to their follow-up appointments.

Step 2 Identify key pain points. Analyze each touchpoint to identify any areas where patients may be encountering challenges, such as long wait times or confusing paperwork.

Step 3 Gather feedback. Talk to patients directly and gather feedback on their experiences with your dental practice. Use this feedback to validate the pain points you have identified and identify any additional areas where you can improve.

Step 4 Prioritize areas for improvement. Based on the feedback and pain points you have identified, prioritize the areas where you can make the most impact.

Step 5 Develop a re-engagement plan. Use the insights from your patient journey analysis to develop a comprehensive re-engagement strategy that addresses the key pain points and prioritizes areas for improvement. This might include tactics such as streamlining processes, improving patient communication, or offering new patient incentives.

In conclusion, building an effective patient re-engagement strategy is critical for any dental practice's success. Dental clinics can customize their strategy to effectively communicate with and re-engage inactive patients by knowing the patient experience. The correct plan can help to win back inactive patients and strengthen the practice's patient base by identifying and evaluating inactive patients, employing technology, and creating clear targets and goals. To give the greatest possible experience and develop long-lasting relationships with patients, it is critical to be proactive, data-driven, and patient-centric. Re-engaging inactive patients can lead to a more robust practice, greater patient outcomes, and increased patient satisfaction if done correctly.

CREATING A SEGMENTED RE-ENGAGEMENT PLAN

To ensure the success of any dental practice, it is essential to re-engage inactive patients. However, with a large patient base, this can be a challenging task. That's why having a well-structured and segmented re-engagement plan is crucial. In this chapter, we will discuss the importance of creating a segmented re-engagement plan, effective methods to segment your inactive patient base, and how to develop a customized plan for each segment. By taking a personalized and targeted approach to re-engaging inactive patients, dental practices can increase the chances of success and make the most of their re-engagement efforts. In the following pages, we will delve into the specific steps and best practices for creating a segmented re-engagement plan tailored to the unique needs and goals of your practice.

Creating a segmented re-engagement plan is a crucial step in effectively re-engaging inactive patients and ensuring the success of a dental practice. By segmenting patients based on their needs and behaviors, practices can tailor their approach and increase the likelihood of success.

Step 1: Identify Patient Segments

The first stage in developing a segmented re-engagement strategy is to identify the various patient segments. This is accomplished by evaluating patient data and metrics in the EMR system and categorizing patients based on their behaviors and needs. For example, one part could be patients who haven't been to the office in over a year, while another could be individuals who have recently moved or changed insurance.

Step 2: Develop Segment-Specific Objectives and Goals

Following the identification of patient segments, the following stage is to define segment-specific objectives and targets for each group. For example, the first segment's goal could be to make appointments for 20% of patients who haven't visited the office in over a year, while the second segment's goal could be to update contact information for 50% of patients who have recently moved or changed insurance.

Step 3: Choose Re-engagement Channels

The next step is to select the most relevant re-engagement channels based on the objectives and goals for each patient segment. For example, a direct mail campaign may be the ideal technique for the first segment, whereas an email campaign may be more beneficial for the second.

Step 4: Develop Segment-Specific Campaigns

Once the re-engagement channels have been chosen, the next step is to develop segment-specific campaigns that are tailored to each group. For example, the direct mail campaign for the first segment may include a personalized letter and appointment scheduling postcard, while the email campaign for the second segment may include a request to update contact information and a thank you for being a valued patient.

Step 5: Monitor and Evaluate Results

The last step in developing a segmented re-engagement strategy is to track and assess the results. This can be accomplished by tracking and comparing response rates for each campaign to objectives and goals. Adjustments to the campaigns can be made based on the results to provide the greatest potential outcomes.

SAMPLE SEGMENTED RE-ENGAGEMENT CAMPAIGN:

PATIENT SEGMENT	PATIENT COUNT	ACTION ITEM	RESPONSIBLE AND DEADLINE	RESULTS
Age > 1 year - No Appointment	1543	Reactivation campaign: Email+SMS +Postcard+ with a cleaning exam Offer on a landing page to schedule appointment at anytime	Outsource and complete the campaign by the end of May.	30 appointments in the last 20 days from the campaign recorded.
No Insurance patients inactive for last 12 months	578	Cash offer on the cleaning services, personalized text messaging campaign	Not assigned	
Unscheduled Treatment Plans in last 12 months	675	Personalized Text and Email Reminders to the patients.	Not Assigned	

CASE STUDY:

A general dentistry used a segmented re-engagement plan to successfully re-engage inactive patients. The practice first identified two patient segments - those who had not visited the practice in over a year and those who had recently moved or changed insurance. The practice then developed segment-specific objectives and goals and chose direct mail and email campaigns as the re-engagement channels. The direct mail campaign for the first segment included a personalized letter and appointment scheduling postcard, while the email campaign for the second segment included a request to update contact information and a thank you for being a valued patient. The practice monitored and evaluated the results and was able to schedule appointments for 25% of patients who had not visited the practice in over a year and update contact information for 60% of patients who had recently moved or changed insurance.

By following these steps, dental practices can create a segmented re-engagement plan that effectively reaches and re-engages inactive patients. By being proactive, data-driven, and patient-centric, practices can strengthen their patient base and provide the best possible experience for patients.

05

COMMUNICATION TOOLS FOR **PATIENT RE-ENGAGEMENT STRATEGY**

- Introduction
- Common Tools for Patient Communication / Personalized Follow-Up
- Sample Messages and Scripts for Personalized Follow-Up
- The Benefits of Reminders and Notifications
- Understanding the Advantages and Disadvantages of Direct Mail
- Sample Direct Mail Messages for Dental Practices

When it comes to patient re-engagement, effective communication is essential. A well-thought-out communication strategy can assist a dental practice in engaging and reactivating inactive patients, resulting in better patient outcomes and more income. With so many communication tools and channels available, it is critical to choose the correct combination of technologies to optimize the impact of your re-engagement plan.

This chapter will look at numerous communication strategies that dentists can use to re-engage inactive patients. From tailored emails and text messages to direct mail and reminders, we will discuss the advantages of each communication medium, as well as sample messages and scripts for each. By the end of this chapter, you will have a thorough understanding of patient re-engagement communication techniques, allowing you to create an effective communication strategy for your dental office.

Personalization is an essential component of a successful patient re-engagement strategy for dentistry practices. In this chapter, we will explore the most frequent routes for personalized follow-up tools, as well as present examples and a case study to demonstrate their effectiveness.

Dental practices can use a variety of channels for personalized follow-up, including email, phone, text messages, and direct mail. Each channel has advantages and disadvantages, and the channel chosen will be determined by criteria such as the target audience, the type of communication, and the available resources.

Note: Sample Emails, Phone scripts, direct mail messaging, Text Messages in this chapter are generated using Chat GPT.

EMAIL	PHONE	TEXT MESSAGES	DIRECT MAIL
Because it allows dental clinics to send tailored messages to patients, email is an ideal avenue for individualized follow-up. Email can be used to send appointment reminders	Personalized phone calls are another effective way to follow up with patients. You can use phone calls to contact patients who have missed appointment	SMS messages are a quick and easy way to contact patients. SMS messages can be used to send appointment reminders	Direct mail is actual mail that is delivered to a patient's house. Appointment reminders

In conclusion, personalized follow-up is a crucial part of a successful patient re-engagement strategy for dental practices. The choice of channel will depend on the target audience, the type of message, and the resources available, but email, phone calls, text messages, and direct mail are all effective options. With the right strategy, personalized follow-up can help dental practices win back their inactive patients and improve their overall patient engagement.

SAMPLE MESSAGES AND SCRIPTS FOR PERSONALIZED FOLLOW-UP

One of the key aspects of utilizing personalized follow-up in patient re-engagement is to craft effective and meaningful messages that can spark interest and encourage patients to return for appointments. In this chapter, we will explore the different types of messages and scripts that dental practices can use for personalized follow-up.

EMAIL MESSAGES

Emails are a convenient and cost-effective way to reach out to patients, and are widely used for personalized follow-up. Here are a few sample email messages that can be used to re-engage inactive patients

Email 1:

Dear [Patient's Name],

I hope this email finds you well. As your dentist, I wanted to reach out to you personally and remind you of the importance of regular dental check-ups for maintaining good oral health. I also wanted to let you know that we miss seeing you at our office and we would love to schedule an appointment for you soon.

If it's been a while since your last appointment, or if you have any dental concerns, we would be more than happy to help. Our team is always here to answer your questions and to make sure that you receive the best possible care.

To schedule an appointment, simply call our office at [Phone Number] or visit our website [Website Link]. We look forward to seeing you soon!

Best regards,

[Your Name]

Email 2:

Subject: [Patient Name]: Don't Neglect Your Oral Health!

Dear [Patient's Name],

As a patient at our dental office, your oral health is important to us. Regular dental check-ups and cleanings are essential for maintaining good oral health and preventing more serious dental problems down the road.

If it's been a while since your last appointment, we encourage you to schedule one soon. Our team is always here to answer any questions you may have and to make sure that you receive the best possible care.

To schedule an appointment, simply call us at [Phone Number] or visit our website [Website Link]. We look forward to seeing you soon!

Best regards,

[Your Name]

Email 3:

Subject: [Patient Name]: Don't Miss Out on Our New Services!

Dear [Patient's Name],

We hope this email finds you well. As a valued patient of our dental office, we wanted to let you know about some exciting new services that we now offer. Whether you're due for a regular check-up or you have a specific dental concern, we have the expertise and the technology to help.

To schedule an appointment and take advantage of our new services, simply call us at [Phone Number] or visit our website [Website Link]. We look forward to seeing you soon!

Best regards,

[Your Name]

Email 4:

Subject: [Patient Name]: A Quick Reminder from Your Dental Office

Dear [Patient's Name],

This is just a quick reminder from your dental office to let you know that it's time for your next appointment. Regular dental check-ups and cleanings are essential for maintaining good oral health, and we would be more than happy to schedule an appointment for you soon.

To schedule an appointment, simply call us at [Phone Number] or visit our website [Website Link]. We look forward to seeing you soon!

Best regards,

[Your Name]

Email 5:

Subject: [Patient Name]: Your Smile is Our Priority!

Dear [Patient's Name],

At our dental office, your smile is our top priority. We believe in providing the best possible dental care to all of our patients, and that starts with regular check-ups and cleanings.

If it's been a while since your last appointment, or if you have any dental concerns, we would be more than happy to help. Our team is always here to answer your questions and to make sure that you receive the best possible care.

To schedule an appointment, simply call us at [Phone Number] or visit our website [Website Link]. We look forward to seeing you soon!

Best regards,

[Your Name]

TEXT MESSAGES

Text messages are a quick and direct way to reach patients, and are becoming increasingly popular for patient re-engagement. Here are a few sample text messages that dental practices can use:

1. *"Hi [Patient's Name], just wanted to check in and see how your oral health is doing. It's been a while since your last appointment, and we'd love to schedule a check-up for you soon. Give us a call at [Phone Number] to book an appointment."*

2. *"Hello [Patient's Name], this is [Your Name] from your dental office. I wanted to reach out and see if you have any concerns or questions about your oral health. We're here to help, so please don't hesitate to give us a call."*

3. *"Good morning [Patient's Name], just wanted to remind you of the importance of regular dental check-ups for maintaining good oral health. It's been a while since your last appointment, so let's schedule one soon! Give us a call at [Phone Number] to book."*

4. *"Hi [Patient's Name], we miss seeing you at our office! If you're due for a check-up or have any dental concerns, we're here to help. Call us at [Phone Number] to schedule an appointment today."*

5. *"Good afternoon [Patient's Name], this is [Your Name] from your dental office. I wanted to reach out and see if there's anything we can do to help with your oral health. Let's schedule a check-up soon! Call us at [Phone Number] to book an appointment."*

PHONE CALLS

Phone calls are a more personal touch, and can be an effective way to re-engage inactive patients. Here are a few sample scripts that dental practices can use for personalized follow-up calls:

1. *Hi [Patient Name], this is [Practice Name]. I'm calling because it's been a while since you've been in for an appointment and I wanted to check in to see if there's anything we can help with.*

2. *[Patient Name], this is [Practice Name]. I noticed that you missed your last appointment and wanted to reach out to see if everything is okay. If there's anything we can do to help, please let us know.*

3. *[Patient Name], this is [Practice Name]. I wanted to touch base with you and see if you're ready to schedule your next appointment. We'd be happy to schedule you now if you're ready.*

DIRECT MAIL/ POSTCARDS:

Postcards are the best way to send personalized direct mail to the patients. These messages are meant to be short, simple, and enticing to encourage inactive patients to schedule appointments. They should be personalized, using the patient's name and addressing their specific needs and concerns. Dental offices can also consider adding eye-catching graphics and images to their postcards to increase their impact and appeal.

Few sample direct mail postcard messages that dental offices can use to bring back inactive patients:

1. *"We Miss You! It's been too long since we've seen your smile. Book your appointment today and receive a complimentary teeth cleaning!"*

2. *"Don't let your dental health slip away. We're here to help! Schedule your appointment today and receive a $50 credit towards your next visit."*

3. *"Your dental health is our top priority. Come back and see us for a check-up, cleaning, and a chance to catch up with our team."*

4. *"We know it's been a while, but we're here to help. Schedule your appointment today and receive a complimentary oral health assessment and consultation."*

5. *"We're committed to helping you achieve your best smile. Schedule your appointment today and receive a free whitening treatment with any dental procedure."*

Direct mail can be a useful tool for dental practices to reach out to inactive patients and bring them back for appointments. However, it is important to weigh the advantages and disadvantages before committing to a direct mail campaign. Dental practices should consider factors such as cost, time, and impact before deciding whether direct mail is the right approach for them.

Personalized follow-up is a crucial component of patient re-engagement, and the messages and scripts outlined above can serve as a starting point for dental practices to craft their own messages that resonate with their patient base. Whether through emails, text messages, or phone calls, it's important to approach personalized follow-up with empathy.

THE BENEFITS OF AUTOMATED REMINDERS AND NOTIFICATIONS:

One of the primary benefits of reminders and notifications is increased patient engagement without your staff having to send text or email manually. By keeping patients informed of upcoming appointments and important information, they are more likely to show up and stay engaged with their dental care. Additionally, reminders and notifications can help reduce the number of missed appointments, which can be costly for both the patient and the practice. In some cases at the dental offices, automated appointment reminders have improved the show rate by 40%.

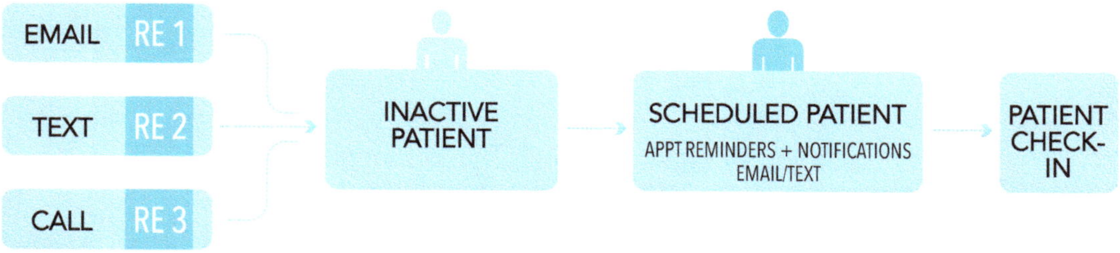

RE: Re-engagement activity

In this chapter, we will explore the most common channels for reminders and notifications, including text messages, email, and automated phone calls, and provide examples of how they can be used to improve patient engagement.

TEXT MESSAGES:

Text messages are one of the most popular channels for reminders and notifications in dental offices. They are fast, convenient, and most people check their phones multiple times a day. To implement automated text messages as a channel for reminders and notifications, dental offices can use automated systems that send out texts to patients a few days before their appointment. These texts can include the date, time, and location of the appointment, as well as any other important information the patient needs to know.

An example of a text message reminder could look like this:

> *"Hello [Patient Name], this is a reminder of your dental appointment on [Date] at [Time]. Please let us know if you need to reschedule or if you have any questions. We look forward to seeing you soon!"*

EMAIL:

Email is another popular channel for reminders and notifications in dental offices. It is a reliable way to reach patients and provide them with important information about their appointments. To implement email as a channel for reminders and notifications, dental offices can use automated systems that send out emails to patients a few days before their appointment. These emails can include the same information as the text messages, such as the date, time, and location of the appointment.

An example of an email reminder could look like this:

> *"Dear [Patient Name],*
>
> *We hope this email finds you well. This is a reminder of your upcoming dental appointment on [Date] at [Time]. We want to make sure you have all the information you need to make the most of your visit. If you need to reschedule or have any questions, please don't hesitate to reach out to us.*
>
> *Thank you for choosing our office for your dental care, and we look forward to seeing you soon.*
>
> *Best regards,*
>
> *[Dental Office Name]"*

AUTOMATED PHONE CALLS:

Automated phone calls are another popular channel for reminders and notifications in dental offices. They are a convenient and effective way to reach patients and ensure they show up for their appointments. To implement automated phone calls as a channel for reminders and notifications, dental offices can use automated systems that make calls to patients a few days before their appointment. These calls can include the same information as the text messages and emails, such as the date, time, and location of the appointment.

An example of an automated phone call reminder could sound like this:

> *"Hello [Patient Name], this is a reminder of your upcoming dental appointment on [Date] at [Time]. Please let us know if you need to reschedule or if you have any questions. We look forward to seeing you soon. Thank you for choosing our office for your dental care."*

CONCLUSION:

In conclusion, there are several common channels for reminders and notifications in dental offices, including text messages, email, and automated phone calls. Each channel has its own strengths and weaknesses, and dental offices should choose the channel that works best for their patients. By using reminders and notifications, dental offices can improve patient engagement and reduce the number of missed appointments, leading to increased patient satisfaction and a positive

Dental practices cannot rely on just one reminder before the appointment day and expect patients to show up. Instead, it is essential to implement a multi-pronged automated message strategy to ensure patients are aware and well-informed. With busy schedules, a single reminder is not enough to capture the patient's attention.

The best practices for reminders and notifications include sending a confirmation message as soon as the appointment is scheduled, followed by reminders three days prior to the appointment, one day before, and even one hour before the appointment. Text messages are best sent before 6 PM in the evening and after 9 AM in the morning, while emails can be sent at any time. By adopting a comprehensive approach to reminders and notifications, dental practices can increase patient engagement and reduce the number of missed appointments.

The results of this strategy have been outstanding. Adopting this approach has improved the show rate by 40% and has improved the overall productivity at the office. By utilizing technology to send reminders and notifications, dental practices can provide better patient care while streamlining their operations.

Here are some sample email and text messages and scripts for dental appointment reminders and notifications, for use three days before the appointment, one day before, and one hour before the appointment:

SAMPLE MESSAGE THAT CAN BE SENT IMMEDIATELY AFTER SCHEDULING AN APPOINTMENT:

Email Subject: Confirmation of Your Dental Appointment

Email Body:

Dear [Patient Name],

We wanted to confirm that you have an appointment scheduled with us at [Dental Practice Name] on [Appointment Date & Time]. We look forward to seeing you soon!

Please make sure to arrive a few minutes early to fill out any necessary forms and to ensure a prompt start to your appointment.

If you need to reschedule or cancel your appointment, please reply to this email or give us a call at [Phone Number].

Best regards,

[Dental Practice Name]

Text Message:

Hi [Patient Name], this is a confirmation of your dental appointment at [Dental Practice Name] on [Appointment Date & Time]. Please arrive a few minutes early. If you need to reschedule or have any questions, please call us at [Phone Number].

3 Days Before the Appointment:

Email Subject: Upcoming Dental Appointment Reminder

Email Body:

Dear [Patient Name],

We wanted to remind you about your upcoming dental appointment at [Dental Practice Name] on [Appointment Date & Time]. We look forward to seeing you soon!

If you need to reschedule or cancel your appointment, please reply to this email or give us a call at [Phone Number].

Best regards,

[Dental Practice Name]

Text Message:

Hi [Patient Name], this is a reminder about your dental appointment at [Dental Practice Name] on [Appointment Date & Time]. If you need to reschedule or have any questions, please call us at [Phone Number].

1 Day Before the Appointment:

Email Subject: Tomorrow's Dental Appointment Reminder

Email Body:

Dear [Patient Name],

Just a friendly reminder about your dental appointment tomorrow at [Dental Practice Name]. We are looking forward to seeing you!

Please make sure to arrive a few minutes early to fill out any necessary forms and to ensure a prompt start to your appointment.

If you need to reschedule or cancel your appointment, please reply to this email or give us a call at [Phone Number].

Best regards,

[Dental Practice Name]

Text Message:

Hi [Patient Name], this is a reminder about your dental appointment tomorrow at [Dental Practice Name]. We recommend arriving a few minutes early. If you need to reschedule or have any questions, please call us at [Phone Number].

1 Hour Before the Appointment:

Email Subject: Final Reminder for Your Dental Appointment Today

Email Body:

Dear [Patient Name],

This is just a final reminder about your dental appointment today at [Dental Practice Name]. We are looking forward to seeing you soon!

If you need to reschedule or cancel your appointment, please reply to this email or give us a call at [Phone Number].

Best regards,

[Dental Practice Name]

Text Message:

Hi [Patient Name], this is a final reminder about your dental appointment today at [Dental Practice Name]. We look forward to seeing you soon! If you need to reschedule or have any questions, please call us at [Phone Number].

CONCLUSION:

With the use of patient communication software, such as mConsent, you can automate the delivery of appointment confirmation messages, eliminating the need for manual intervention by your staff

06

IMPLEMENTING AND **ACHIEVING** RESULTS

Effective patient re-engagement strategies can help dental practices to reactivate inactive patients, reduce patient churn, and generate new business. However, implementing a successful patient re-engagement strategy requires careful planning, execution, and tracking. In this chapter, we will discuss some key tips for implementing a patient re-engagement strategy that delivers solid results.

KEY POINTS:

1. **Use multiple communication tools:** There is no single communication tool that will provide you with the best outcomes. Use a combination of technologies like email, text messaging, phone calls, direct mail, and social media to optimize the success of your patient re-engagement activities. You can attain the finest results by employing all of these tools in tandem.

2. **Use personalized messaging and offers:** Personalization is key to effective patient re-engagement. Use personalized emails, text messages, and direct mail that speak directly to the patient and offer something of value, such as a special offer, a reason to book an appointment now, or a sense of urgency.

3. **Design a landing page that converts:** When patients respond to your messaging, it's important to have a solid landing page that encourages them to book an appointment. This landing page should be visually appealing, feature testimonials and social proof, provide a solid offer, and include a clear call to action.

4. **Outsource to a professional:** Re-engaging patients can be a laborious and difficult process. Take into account contracting out your patient re-engagement initiatives to a reputable business with a focus on dental marketing. You can obtain expert assistance from a company to create a focused, successful re-engagement strategy and track your results to make sure you are getting the optimum ROI.

CASE STUDY:

HOW A DENTAL OFFICE BOOKED 40 APPOINTMENTS EACH MONTH.

A dental practice Crescent Family Dental in the Chicago suburbs was purchased as an additional location by a doctor. The practice had been in business for over three years and had a database of approximately 2,500 patients with email addresses and phone numbers. The website was old and needed a revamp, but the practice had a 5-star Google rating with 50 reviews.

The doctor had a choice after purchasing the practice to either invest in marketing for new patients or implement a re-engagement strategy for patients who had been to the practice before. The practice decided to focus on re-engaging with inactive patients, rather than spending money on attracting new patients.

After deciding to focus on reengaging with inactive patients, the dental practice embarked on a step-by-step process to design and implement a successful patient reengagement campaign.

Step 1: Analyze Inactive Patients in the EMR System

The first step was to analyze the inactive patients in the EMR system to determine the total number of patients who had not visited the practice in the past six months. The practice identified a total of 2,500 inactive patients.

Step 2: Categorize the Inactive Patients

The practice then categorized the inactive patients based on their last visit dates, family size, employer type, and insurance. This helped the practice to create a segmented re-engagement plan that targeted each group of patients with personalized messages.

Step 3: Cold Emails and Text Designed to Re-Engage with a Solid Offer

The mConsent team helped practice then design personalized cold emails and text messages to re-engage with the inactive patients. The messages included a solid offer that was designed to get the patients to schedule an appointment ASAP.

Step 4: Landing Page Designed with Solid Offer, CTA, and Testimonials

To further encourage the inactive patients to book an appointment, the practice created a landing page that included a solid offer, a clear call-to-action, and testimonials from satisfied patients. The landing page also showcased the practice's 5-star Google reviews. The patients knew the deadline to take up the offer, and emails and SMS were designed to remind them of the offer.

Step 5: The practice wanted to ensure that the inactive

patients received an email introducing the new doctor and the staff, followed by multiple reminders of the offer to encourage them to come back to the office for an appointment. As a result, they designed postcards with the same offer and call-to-action as the emails and text messages.

The postcards were sent out to the 2,500 inactive patients a total of three times over a period of three months. Each postcard was designed to grab the attention of the patient and remind them of the offer that was available to them.

In addition to the offer, the postcards also included a tracking mechanism. Patients were asked to bring the postcard with them to their appointment to track the impact of the postcard marketing. This allowed the practice to determine which postcard designs were most effective and which ones needed to be improved.

The postcard campaign was a success, with many patients responding positively and coming back to the office for an appointment. The tracking mechanism also allowed the practice to see which postcard designs were most effective and make adjustments for future campaigns.

Overall, the postcard campaign was an important part of the re-engagement strategy and helped to bring many inactive patients back to the practice.

Step 6: Facebook Retargeting Designed with an Offer

The social media strategy of the re-engagement campaign was crucial in reminding patients about the offer and encouraging them to schedule an appointment. The practice utilized Facebook retargeting to target those who had visited the landing page in the last 30 days.

The retargeting ads were designed with eye-catching images and a clear message to remind patients about the offer and encourage them to schedule an appointment. The practice also created a video ad that helped to explain the offer.

The retargeting ads were effective in bringing patients back to the landing page and booking appointments through the online scheduling tool. The practice saw an increase in online appointment bookings and an overall increase in appointment bookings through all channels.

The use of video in the retargeting ads was particularly effective in capturing the attention of potential patients and communicating the value of the practice. The video was short and to the point, highlighting the benefits of the practice and the offer available to re-engaged patients.

Step 7: The practice added a strategy to gather fresh

and latest Google reviews from patients using reputation management tools. This was designed to build trust in the practice among potential patients who were researching online. The strategy involved sending automated review requests to patients after their appointments, making it easy for them to leave a review. This helped to boost the number of positive reviews for the practice and build more social proof online. The practice continued to monitor and respond to reviews regularly to maintain a positive online reputation.

Step 8: Incorporating Online Appointment Scheduling

To make the appointment booking process more efficient, the practice incorporated an online appointment scheduling system. Patients could book their appointments directly from the practice's website without having to make a phone call.

However, the study found that while many patients appreciated the convenience of online scheduling, a significant portion still preferred to call and speak with a human to set up their appointment. Despite this, online scheduling helped those who scheduled themselves during non-business hours.

The incorporation of online scheduling allowed for more efficient use of staff time and made it easier for patients to book appointments at their convenience.

The practice outsourced the re-engagement strategy to a professional company (mConsent in this case), which incorporated social media and direct mailing into the mix. The strategy generated 40 appointments in the first month and has since continued to bring in an additional 40-60 appointments each month. The ROI was 5 times the investment within 6 months.

Overall, the re-engagement strategy proved to be a successful approach for the practice in booking appointments and building trust with patients. The use of available technology and online scheduling helped the office to book appointments efficiently, especially during times when they were short-staffed.

Below is the chart of the overall Patient Re-engagement Strategy that was implemented at the Practice.

Overall Re-Engagement Strategy at Crescent Family Dental

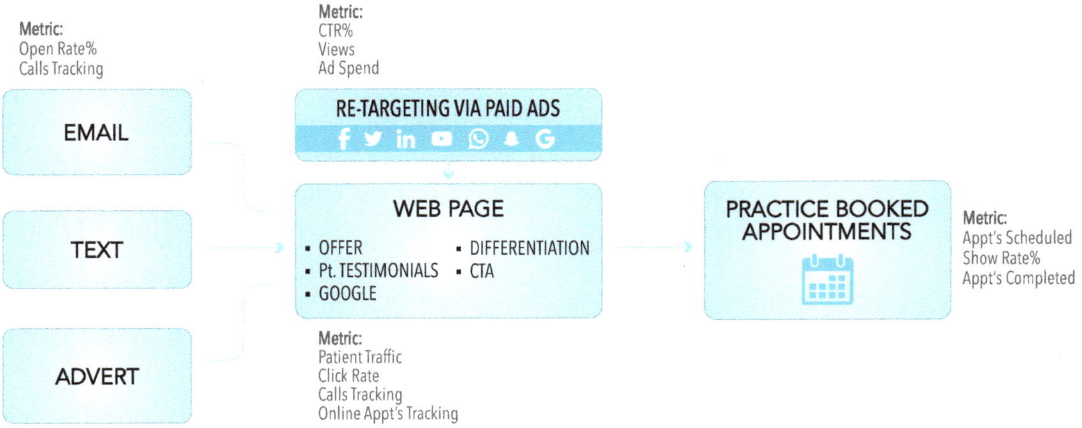

Plan 2:
Patient Engagement Plan without Landing Page

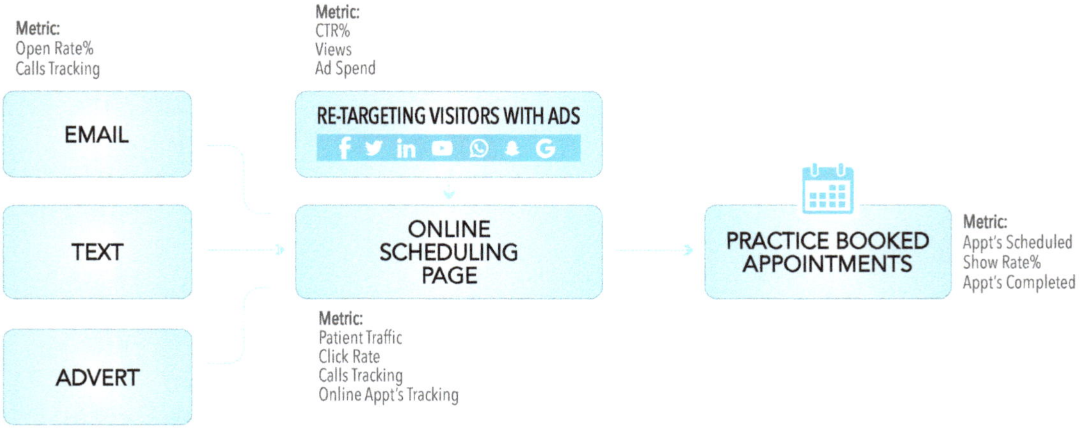

Re-Engagement Communication Plan

Day	1	2	3	4	4	5	6	7	8	9	10	11	12	13	14	15
Patient Category	C1			C2			C3			C4			C5			
Email Type	Email 1	Email 2	Email 3	Email 1	Email 2	Email 3	Email 1	Email 2	Email 3	Email 1	Email 2	Email 3	Email 1	Email 2	Email 3	
SMS	SMS 1	SMS 2	SMS 3	SMS 1	SMS 2	SMS 3	SMS 1	SMS 2	SMS 3	SMS 1	SMS 2	SMS 3	SMS 1	SMS 2	SMS 3	
Post Card Delivery																Target Post Card Delivery

Patient Category	Inactive Patients
(C1)	300
(C2)	320
(C3)	210
(C4)	321
(C5)	370

In conclusion, the success of this case study illustrates the importance of a well-planned and executed patient re-engagement strategy. By using a multi-channel approach, personalized messaging and offers, and data analytics, this dental practice was able to achieve a high ROI and improve the overall patient experience. By partnering with a professional dental marketing company, they were able to achieve even better results and continuously refine their strategy over time. The addition of a new website design and patient review strategy also played a crucial role in building trust with patients and improving the overall patient experience.

TESTIMONIAL FROM CRESCENT FAMILY DENTAL:

mConsent

Write a review

6160, Summit Drive North, STE355 Brooklyn Center, Minneapolis, MN

4.8 ★★★★★ 21 reviews

Most relevant | Newest | Highest | Lowest

Syed Sharief
2 reviews

★★★★★ 6 days ago NEW

I am thrilled to endorse the mConsent team for their invaluable insights and hands-on support that have greatly benefited our dental practice, Crescent Family Dental. They introduced us to their innovative patient re-engagement approach, which has been remarkably successful, leading to a substantial increase in patient appointments. Their continuous assistance ensured we were fully on-boarded with tools for going paperless, appointment reminders, patient messaging, and reputation management. The mConsent team has consistently delivered exceptional guidance, support, and customer service, while offering a user-friendly platform. Their patient re-engagement solution has revolutionized our practice, optimizing our workflow and eliminating the need for manual reminders. I wholeheartedly recommend mConsent's patient re-engagement solution to any dental practice aiming to enhance patient engagement and retention. Thank you, mConsent, for assisting us in expanding our practice and better serving our patients!
Bilal Shareef- Office Manager

2

07

IMPROVING **PATIENT EXPERIENCE**

Introduction: Any dental office's success depends on how satisfied its patients are. A positive patient experience can keep current patients and attract new ones. On the other hand, a negative patient experience may cause the patient to become dissatisfied and seek care elsewhere. Dental practices must place a high priority on improving the patient experience in order to re-engage inactive patients.

PHYSICIAN / DENTIST

Primary Patient Contact and relationship
Applies to Dentist Owner & Associate

1. Adequate and relevant training:
   - Management tools
   - Patient Satisfaction tools
   - Payment Models
2. Autonomy to manage patients quality of life
3. Leadership skill development

PERSONNEL

Hygienist, Dental Assistant, Office Manager, Treatment Plan Coordinator

1. Skill development and training:
   - Emotional residency
   - Empathy
   - Customer service training
2. Access to Mentors
3. Patients and patient expectations

PLACES

Alternative Access Point

1. Connecting people and patient in the appropriate places
2. Optimally matched with patients conditions and preferences
3. Use of telemedicine when appropriate

PROCESSES

Effective, Efficient, Timely and Safe

1. Patient centered: matched to patient sub-segments
2. Informed by newest models of operations management research
3. Designed with patient customer perspective in mind

THE IMPORTANCE OF PATIENT EXPERIENCE:

The patient experience is the sum of all interactions a patient has with a dental office, from the first phone call to the final checkout. It plays a critical role in the success of a dental practice, as satisfied patients are more likely to return for future appointments, recommend the practice to friends and family, and become long-term patients.

Therefore, it's essential for dental offices to prioritize and continually improve the patient experience. The following patient experience checklist serves as a guide for dental offices looking to enhance their patients' overall experience.

1. Physicians (Dentist/Dentist Associates):

- Building a rapport with patients and taking the time to get to know them, their dental history, and their goals for their oral health
- Explaining procedures and treatments in a clear, concise, and easy-to-understand manner
- Providing follow-up care and support, including answering questions and addressing concerns
- Providing associate dentists with the autonomy to manage patients, including making treatment decisions and communicating with patients
- Ensuring that associate dentists have access to the management tools and resources they need to provide high-quality, efficient care

2. Personnel/Staff:

- Providing friendly, helpful, and professional support throughout the patient's visit
- Making sure that the patient is comfortable and at ease, for example by offering a wifi password while waiting or a glass of water

- Maintaining a clean and organized practice environment to help patients feel more at ease

- Training staff members on emotional resilience to help them maintain a positive and compassionate attitude, even in challenging situations

- Providing empathy training to help staff members understand and connect with the emotions and experiences of patients

- Offering customer service training to help staff members understand the importance of creating a positive and welcoming experience for patients, and to give them the skills and tools they need to provide exceptional customer service.

3. Processes:

- Implementing efficient systems for scheduling appointments and managing patient flow

- Providing clear and concise information about treatments, procedures, and expected outcomes

- Using technology, such as digital X-rays or patient portals, to streamline the care process and improve communication with patients

- Going paperless at check-in, using electronic forms and digital signatures to streamline the intake process

- Making appointment setting easier, for example by offering online scheduling, flexible appointment times, or same-day appointments

- Implementing a text-to-pay system to make it easier for patients to pay their bills and manage their finances

- Streamlining processes within the practice, such as using electronic health records, automated appointment reminders, and efficient communication systems to improve patient flow and reduce wait times.

4. Place:

- Providing a welcoming, clean, and comfortable clinic environment that makes patients feel at ease
- Ensuring that the clinic is easily accessible and located in a convenient location for patients, with ample parking and public transportation options
- Making the clinic easy to find, with clear signage, well-lit pathways, and a user-friendly website that provides directions and contact information
- Providing a patient-centered design that maximizes comfort and minimizes stress, for example by offering plush seating, relaxing lighting, and calming music
- Creating a warm and inviting atmosphere, for example by using natural materials, soft colors, and friendly artwork or decorations
- Investing in the latest equipment and technologies to provide state-of-the-art care and help patients feel confident in the care they are receiving.

By putting the needs of their patients first and providing an effective, efficient, and timely service, dentists may foster trust, loyalty, and positive connections with their patients. The following 12 question checklist can help dental offices provide a satisfying patient experience.

Reference: The four Ps of patient experience: A new strategic framework informed by theory and practice

https://www.researchgate.net/publication/329689637_The_four_Ps_of_patient_experience_A_new_strategic_framework_informed_by_theory_and_practice

CREATING A POSITIVE PATIENT EXPERIENCE: A 12 QUESTIONS INTERNAL CHECKLIST FOR DENTAL PRACTICES

1. **Accessibility:** Does the dental clinic have easy accessibility and parking for patients, as well as facilities that are accessible?

2. **Scheduling:** Are there flexible and easy-to-use scheduling options available for patients, such as online booking and reminder notifications?

3. **Check-In and Waiting Room Experience:** Is the check-in process quick and efficient, and is the waiting room comfortable and welcoming?

4. **Care Delivery:** Does the dental practice deliver high-quality, personalized care, and are patients informed and involved in their treatment plans?

5. **Follow-Up and Communication:** Does the dental practice provide timely follow-up and communicate effectively with patients, both during and after appointments?

6. **Service and Support:** Does the dental practice provide excellent customer service, and is support available for patients with questions or concerns?

7. **Personalized Communication:** Do we personalize all forms of communication, including email, text, and phone calls? Do we address patients by name in our communications? Are all communications friendly, professional, and engaging?

8. **On-Time Appointments:** Do we start and end appointments on time? Do we show respect for patients' schedules and minimize wait times?

9. **Clean and Comfortable Environment:** Is our office clean, well-maintained, and welcoming? Do we provide comfortable seating and entertainment for patients?

10. **Clear Explanations:** Do we provide clear and concise explanations of procedures, treatments, and costs? Are patients fully informed and comfortable with their dental care?

11. **Listening to Patients:** Do we actively listen to patients? Do we acknowledge their concerns and questions? Do we provide answers in a timely manner?

12. **Overall Satisfaction:** Do patients feel satisfied with their experiences at the dental practice, and are they likely to recommend the practice to others?

In summary, the patient experience is a crucial component of a successful dental practice. By adhering to the guidelines presented in this chapter, dental practices can establish a positive patient experience that not only boosts patient satisfaction but also results in higher patient retention, referrals, and ultimately practice growth. The patient experience checklist provides a practical framework for evaluating the current patient experience and identifying areas for improvement. By prioritizing accessibility, scheduling, check-in and waiting room experience, care delivery, follow-up and communication, service and support, personalized communication, on-time appointments, a clean and comfortable environment, clear explanations, listening to patients, and overall satisfaction, dental practices can establish a patient-centric culture that emphasizes excellent care and customer service. By making patient experience a critical performance indicator, dental practices can differentiate themselves in a competitive market and build lasting relationships with patients.

IDENTIFYING OPPORTUNITIES TO IMPROVE PATIENT EXPERIENCE AT YOUR PRACTICE:

Introduction:

Giving patients a satisfying experience has become crucial to the healthcare sector as a whole, including the dental sector. It can aid dental practices in growing their clientele, building a solid reputation in the neighborhood, and ensuring their long-term success. Dental offices must be proactive in identifying and resolving areas where the patient experience can be enhanced if they are to achieve this. To help dental practices assess their current operations and spot potential areas for development, the following checklist has been developed.

Step 1: Conduct a Patient Experience Survey

To improve the patient experience, dental clinics should start by soliciting input from their present patients. One successful strategy is to carry out a survey using online forms, phone interviews, or live focus groups. The survey should seek comments on certain aspects of the practice, such as the doctor, personnel, procedures, and location, as well as the patient's overall experience.

Step 2: Analyze the Results

Once the survey results are collected, they should be analyzed to identify areas of strength and areas that need improvement. For example, if patients consistently rate the clinic staff as friendly and helpful, this is a strength that can be highlighted in marketing materials. However, if patients are dissatisfied with the wait time or the efficiency of the check-in process, these are areas that need improvement.

Step 3: Use the Checklist to Identify Opportunities for Improvement

Dental offices should use the checklist for enhancing patient experience to pinpoint specific areas that require improvement after conducting a patient experience survey. Four main categories—physician, personnel, processes, and location—are included in the checklist. For instance, if patients complain that the check-in process is inefficient, the dentist office can review the procedure and make modifications to improve efficiency and cut down on wait times. Dental offices can develop a more patient-centered approach to their services and improve the overall patient experience by using the survey results in conjunction with the checklist.

Step 4: Implement Changes and Reassess

Once opportunities for improvement have been identified, the next step is to implement changes and reassess the patient experience. This may involve retraining staff, updating processes, investing in new technology, or making physical changes to the clinic environment. The reassessment should be done through another patient experience survey to determine the effectiveness of the changes and identify any additional areas for improvement.

Conclusion:

Improving patient experience is an ongoing effort that demands commitment and dedication from the entire dental clinic team. Utilizing a patient experience survey and the checklist for improving patient experience, dental offices can pinpoint areas for growth and implement changes to create a more positive and remarkable experience for patients. This approach can assist in attracting new patients, building a solid reputation in the community, and guaranteeing long-term prosperity in the healthcare industry.

SAMPLE SURVEY QUESTIONS FOR DENTAL OFFICE TO UNDERSTAND THE PATIENT EXPERIENCE:

1. On a scale of 1 to 10, how would you rate the overall friendliness of our front desk staff?
2. Was the wait time for your appointment reasonable?
3. Was our office clean and well-maintained?
4. Was the dental equipment and technology up-to-date and modern?
5. Did you feel informed and well-educated about your dental treatment options?
6. Was the pricing and payment process clear and straightforward?
7. Was the dental care you received high-quality and effective?
8. Were your needs and comfort a priority during the appointment?
9. How would you rate the communication between our staff and yourself during the appointment?
10. Would you recommend our dental office to a friend or family member?
11. Is there anything else you would like to share about your experience at our dental office?
12. May we use your feedback for future improvements and marketing purposes?
13. How likely are you to schedule another appointment at our office in the future?
14. Would you like to be contacted for follow-up regarding your experience? If so, please provide your contact information.

Conclusion: Improving the patient experience is crucial for dental practices looking to re-engage inactive patients. By incorporating a number of key strategies, including personalized communication, convenient scheduling, advanced technology, a comfortable environment, clear explanations, and follow-up care, dental practices can create a positive experience that will keep patients coming back.

08

MEASURING AND EVALUATING **RE-ENGAGEMENT EFFORTS**

UNDERSTANDING KEY PERFORMANCE INDICATORS

Introduction: Re-engagement efforts are essential for dental offices that want to retain patients and improve their overall performance. However, it's important to measure and evaluate these efforts to ensure that they're effective. Key performance indicators (KPIs) can help dental offices track their re-engagement efforts and identify areas for improvement.

KPI's FOR RE-ENGAGEMENT EFFORTS:

1. **Appointment attendance rate:** This KPI measures the percentage of patients who attend their scheduled appointments. A low appointment attendance rate may indicate a lack of patient engagement or dissatisfaction with the clinic's services.

   Suppose a dental office has 100 appointments scheduled for the week, but only 80 patients showed up for their appointments. The Appointment Attendance Rate for the week would be:

   Appointment Attendance Rate = (Number of attended appointments / Total number of scheduled appointments) x 100%

   Appointment Attendance Rate = (80 / 100) x 100% = 80%

   So the Appointment Attendance Rate for that week would be 80%. The dental office could use this KPI to monitor the attendance rate over time and identify any patterns or trends that could indicate a need to implement new re-engagement strategies or reminders to ensure that patients attend their appointments.

2. Patient satisfaction rate: This KPI measures the percentage of patients who are satisfied with the services provided by the clinic. A low patient satisfaction rate may indicate a need for improvement in customer service or other areas.

Patient Satisfaction Rate = (Number of satisfied patients / Total number of patients) x 100%

For example, if a dental office has 100 patients and 85 of them report being satisfied with the services provided, the calculation would be:

Patient Satisfaction Rate = (85 / 100) x 100% = 85%

So the patient satisfaction rate for that dental office would be 85%

3. Referral rate: This KPI measures the percentage of patients who refer friends or family to the clinic. A low referral rate may indicate a lack of patient engagement or dissatisfaction with the clinic's services.

To collect and measure the referral rate, dental offices can use the following steps:

1. Track the number of new patients who come to the clinic as a result of referrals from existing patients.

2. Calculate the total number of patients who visit the clinic during a specific time period (for example, a month).

3. Divide the number of new patients who came to the clinic through referrals by the total number of patients during the same time period.

4. Multiply the result by 100 to get the referral rate as a percentage.

Here's an example:

Suppose a dental office had 100 new patients in a month, and 20 of them were referred by existing patients. The total number of patients who visited the clinic in that month was 500. To calculate the referral rate:

Referral Rate = (Number of new patients from referrals / Total number of patients) x 100%

Referral Rate = (20 / 500) x 100% = 4%

So the referral rate for that month would be 4%.

By tracking the referral rate over time, dental offices can evaluate the effectiveness of their referral program and identify ways to improve it. They can also use this KPI to measure patient satisfaction and engagement, as patients who are satisfied with their experience at the clinic are more likely to refer others.

4. Treatment plan acceptance rate: This KPI measures the percentage of patients who accept the recommended treatment plan. A low treatment plan acceptance rate may indicate a lack of patient engagement or dissatisfaction with the clinic's services.

To measure and track the Treatment Plan Acceptance Rate, dental offices can follow these steps:

1. Keep track of the total number of treatment plans presented to patients during a given time period (for example, a month).

2. Determine the number of treatment plans that were accepted by patients during that same time period.

3. Divide the number of accepted treatment plans by the total number of treatment plans presented.

4. Multiply the result by 100 to get the Treatment Plan Acceptance Rate as a percentage.

Here's an example:

Suppose a dental office presented a total of 50 treatment plans to patients in a month and 30 of those plans were accepted by patients. To calculate the Treatment Plan Acceptance Rate:

Treatment Plan Acceptance Rate = (Number of accepted treatment plans / Total number of presented treatment plans) x 100%

Treatment Plan Acceptance Rate = (30 / 50) x 100% = 60%

So the Treatment Plan Acceptance Rate for that month would be 60%.

By tracking the Treatment Plan Acceptance Rate over time, dental offices can evaluate the effectiveness of their treatment planning process and identify areas for improvement. If the acceptance rate is low, the office may need to consider different methods for presenting treatment plans or improve their communication with patients about the recommended treatments. By improving the Treatment Plan Acceptance Rate, dental offices can improve patient outcomes and increase revenue.

HERE'S HOW TO GENERATE REPORTS FOR TREATMENT PLAN ACCEPTANCE RATE IN DENTRIX, EAGLESOFT, AND OPEN DENTAL:

1. **Dentrix:** In Dentrix, you can generate a Treatment Acceptance Report by going to Office Manager > Treatment Planner > Treatment Acceptance. This report provides a list of all treatment plans presented to patients along with the status of each plan (accepted, rejected, pending, etc.) and the date it was presented. You can then use this information to calculate the Treatment Plan Acceptance Rate as described in the previous answer.

2. **Eaglesoft:** In Eaglesoft, you can generate a Treatment Plan Presentation Report by going to Reports > Marketing > Treatment Plan Presentation. This report provides a list of all treatment plans presented to patients, along with the date, provider, and status of each plan. You can then use this information to calculate the Treatment Plan Acceptance Rate as described in the previous answer.

3. **Open Dental:** In Open Dental, you can generate a Treatment Plan Presentation Report by going to Reports > Treatment Plan > Treatment Plan Presentation. This report provides a list of all treatment plans presented to patients, along with the date, provider, and status of each plan. You can then use this information to calculate the Treatment Plan Acceptance Rate as described in the previous answer.

4. **Patient retention rate:** This KPI measures the percentage of patients who continue to use the clinic's services over time. A low patient retention rate may indicate a need for improvement in customer service or other areas.

Determine the total number of active patients at the beginning of a specific time period (for example, a month).

Determine the number of patients who returned to the clinic for a subsequent visit during that same time period.

Divide the number of returning patients by the total number of active patients at the beginning of the time period.

Multiply the result by 100 to get the patient retention rate as a percentage.

Here's an example:

Suppose a dental office had 500 active patients at the beginning of the month, and 450 of those patients returned for a subsequent visit during the same month. To calculate the patient retention rate:

Patient Retention Rate = (Number of returning patients / Total number of active patients) x 100%

Patient Retention Rate = (450 / 500) x 100% = 90%

So the patient retention rate for that month would be 90%.

Here's how to generate reports for patient retention rate in Dentrix, Eaglesoft, and Open Dental:

1. **Dentrix:** In Dentrix, you can generate a Recall Report by going to Office Manager > Lists > Recall. This report provides a list of all patients who are due for a recall appointment, along with their contact information and the date of their last visit. You can use this report to track patient retention by comparing the number of active patients from one recall period to the next. The difference between the number of active patients in each period divided by the starting number will give you the patient retention rate.

2. **Eaglesoft:** In Eaglesoft, you can generate a Patient Reactivation Report by going to Reports > Management > Patient Reactivation. This report provides a list of all patients who have not been to the clinic in a specified time period, along with their contact information and last visit date. You can use this report to identify patients who have not returned for a subsequent visit and implement targeted re-engagement strategies to encourage them to come back.

3. **Open Dental:** In Open Dental, you can generate a Recall Report by going to Reports > Recall > Recall Report. This report provides a list of all patients who are due for a recall appointment, along with their contact information and the date of their last visit. You can use this report to track patient retention by comparing the number of active patients from one recall period to the next. The difference between the number of active patients in each period divided by the starting number will give you the patient retention rate.

By tracking the patient retention rate over time, dental offices can evaluate the effectiveness of their patient retention strategies and identify areas for improvement. They can also use this KPI to measure patient satisfaction and engagement, as patients who are satisfied with their experience at the clinic are more likely to return for future visits. Additionally, dental offices can identify patients who have not returned for a subsequent visit and implement targeted re-engagement strategies to encourage them to come back.

EVALUATION OF RE-ENGAGEMENT EFFORTS:

To evaluate the effectiveness of re-engagement efforts, dental offices can use the KPIs listed above. By tracking these KPIs over time, dental offices can identify trends and areas for improvement. For example, if the appointment attendance rate is consistently low, the clinic may need to implement new appointment reminders or other re-engagement strategies.

In addition to tracking KPIs, dental offices can also conduct patient satisfaction surveys and focus groups to gain additional feedback from patients. These surveys and focus groups can provide valuable insights into patient satisfaction and areas for improvement. By focusing on re-engagement efforts and improving the patient experience, dental offices can increase patient retention and ensure that their patients are satisfied with the services provided.

Conclusion:

Measuring and evaluating re-engagement efforts is crucial for dental offices that want to retain patients and improve their overall performance. By tracking KPIs, including appointment attendance rate, patient satisfaction rate, referral rate, treatment plan acceptance rate, and patient retention rate, dental offices can identify trends and areas for improvement. By continuously evaluating and improving their re-engagement efforts, dental offices can provide a positive and memorable experience for their patients while improving their overall performance.

TRACKING RE-ENGAGEMENT SUCCESS: UNDERSTANDING KEY PERFORMANCE INDICATORS

Tracking re-engagement success is important for dental offices to determine the effectiveness of their re-engagement strategies and identify areas for improvement. Here are some key steps to track re-engagement success:

1. **Set a goal:** The first step in tracking re-engagement success is to set a specific goal for what you want to achieve with your re-engagement efforts. This could be increasing patient retention, improving appointment attendance rates, or increasing treatment plan acceptance rates.

2. **Identify key metrics:** Once you have set a goal, identify the key metrics you will use to track your progress. This could include patient retention rate, appointment attendance rate, treatment plan acceptance rate, and referral rate.

3. **Monitor progress:** Regularly track your progress towards your goal by collecting data on your key metrics. Use your practice management software to generate reports on patient retention, appointment attendance, treatment plan acceptance, and other relevant data.

4. **Analyze the data:** After gathering data, evaluate it to detect any trends or patterns. Look for areas where you are making progress and areas where you could improve.

5. **Adjust strategies:** Based on your analysis, adjust your re-engagement strategies as needed. For example, if you are not seeing the desired results with a particular strategy, try a different approach or adjust your messaging.

6. **Continuously improve:** Finally, continuously evaluate and improve your re-engagement strategies based on your results. As you implement new strategies, track their effectiveness and make adjustments as needed.

By tracking re-engagement success, dental offices can improve patient engagement, increase revenue, and provide better care to their patients. With a data-driven approach to re-engagement, dental offices can identify areas for improvement and continually optimize their re-engagement strategies.

HERE ARE SOME OF THE KEY TOOLS AND RESOURCES THAT DENTAL OFFICES CAN USE TO TRACK RE-ENGAGEMENT SUCCESS:

1. **Practice management software:** Most practice management software includes reporting and analytics features that can be used to track key metrics such as patient retention, appointment attendance, and treatment plan acceptance. Dentrix, Eaglesoft, and Open Dental are examples of popular practice management software used in dental offices.

2. **Customer relationship management (CRM) software:** A CRM system can help dental offices track patient interactions, follow-up tasks, and marketing campaigns. HubSpot, Salesforce, and Zoho are examples of popular CRM software that can be customized for use in dental offices.

3. **Patient surveys:** Surveys can be a valuable tool for collecting feedback from patients about their experience with the dental office. This feedback can be used to identify areas for improvement and track changes in patient satisfaction over time. mConsent is a patient engagement software that can be used for patient surveys and to manage patient forms and consent.

4 **Paperless Software:** By adopting paperless solutions, dental offices can greatly improve their efficiency and organizational capabilities. They can effortlessly send patient documents via email or text before appointments, making the entire process more streamlined and convenient for both the patients and the dental practice.

5 **Appointment reminder software:** Automated appointment reminders can help reduce no-shows and improve appointment attendance rates. Many practice management software systems include this feature, and there are also standalone appointment reminder tools available such as Lighthouse 360, Solutionreach, and mConsent.

6 **Referral tracking software:** Referral tracking software can help dental offices track referrals from existing patients and measure the success of their referral programs.

7 **Call tracking software:** Call tracking software can help dental offices monitor and analyze incoming phone calls to improve patient communication and identify opportunities for improvement. MangoVoice is a useful tool to track the incoming calls.

8 **Reputation management software:** Reputation management software can be used to monitor and respond to patient reviews and feedback online. This can help dental offices improve their online reputation and identify areas for improvement. mConsent is an example of a reputation management software that dental offices can use to manage patient feedback and online reputation.

By using these tools and resources, dental offices can evaluate the effectiveness of their patient re-engagement strategies, identify areas for improvement, and continuously optimize their patient engagement and re-engagement efforts.

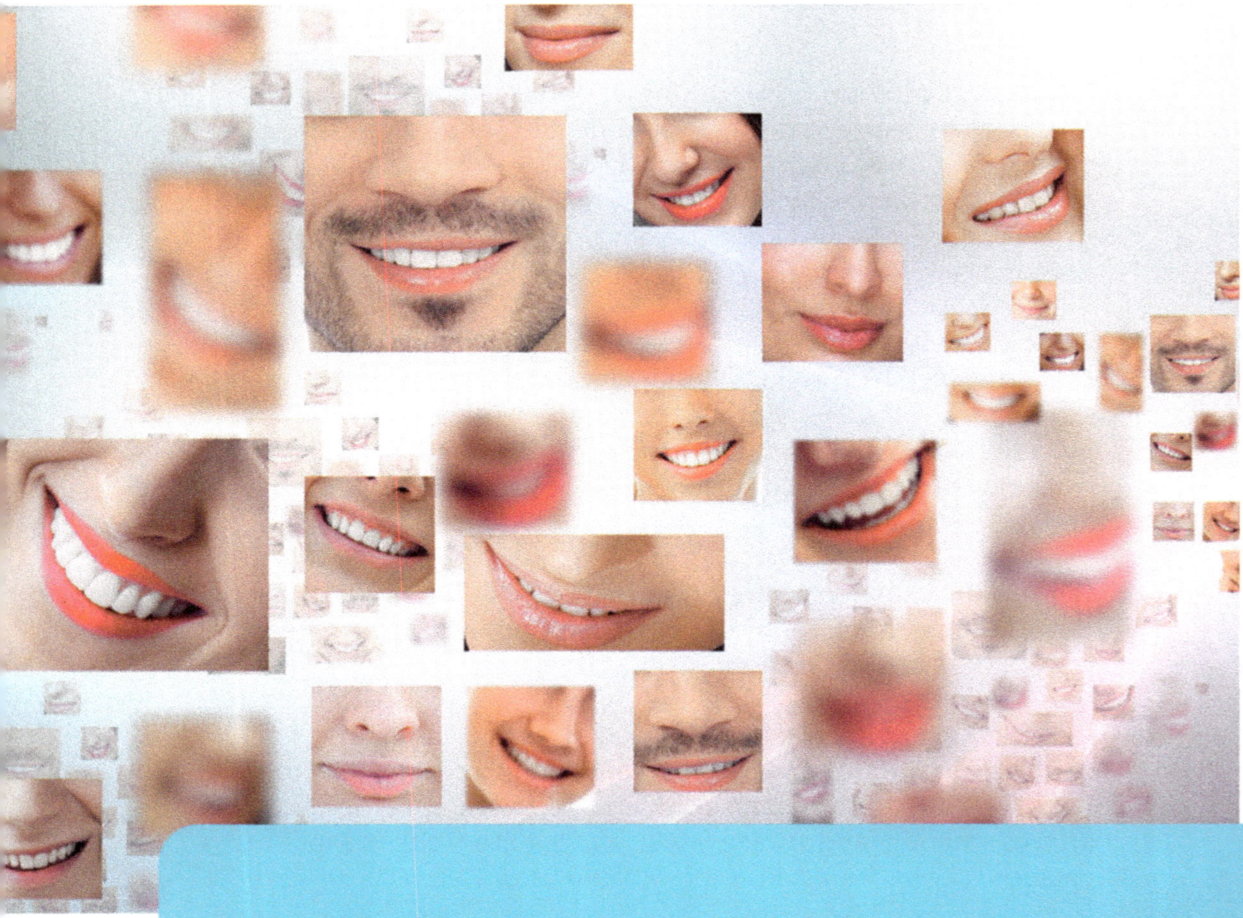

09

THE ART OF PATIENT RE-ENGAGEMENT – **A PATH TO SUCCESS** FOR DENTAL PRACTICES

Introduction:

Dental practices must focus on patient retention and engagement since these factors are essential to their success. Re-engagement is the process of getting in touch with patients who have been inactive for a while or have missed appointments. Dental practices can reduce the chance of losing these consumers, improve patient retention, and expand their clientele by reengaging them. The importance of patient re-engagement, the best ways to apply patient re-engagement techniques, and the prospects for patient re-engagement in dentistry offices are highlighted in this chapter.

IMPORTANCE OF PATIENT RE-ENGAGEMENT:

Patient re-engagement is critical for dental practices as it has a significant impact on patient retention and practice growth. The following are the reasons why patient re-engagement is essential:

1. Enhancing Patient Experience: Patient re-engagement helps enhance the patient experience. Patients who receive regular communication and follow-ups from their dental practice feel more valued and engaged. Dental practices that prioritize patient engagement and communication build patient trust, loyalty, and satisfaction.

2. Retaining Patients: Retaining existing patients is a cost-effective strategy for dental practices. Patient re-engagement is an essential aspect of this strategy, as it helps to reduce the risk of losing patients, increase patient retention, and improve practice revenue. Compared to acquiring new patients, re-engaging existing ones is easier and more cost-effective. This chapter explores the importance of patient re-engagement, best practices for patient re-engagement, and the future of patient re-engagement in dental practices.

3. Building Patient Loyalty: Patient re-engagement helps build patient loyalty. Patients who receive personalized communication and follow-ups from their dental practice are more likely to stay loyal to their dentist. Patient loyalty leads to patient referrals, positive reviews, and practice growth.

FUTURE OF PATIENT RE-ENGAGEMENT:

Re-engaging patients is anticipated to be crucial to the success of dental clinics in the future. The following new developments will influence patient re-engagement in the future:

1. Personalization through Artificial Intelligence: AI-powered systems such as chatbots can provide personalized and conversational experiences for patients, reducing the administrative burden on dental staff.

2. Tele-dentistry: Tele-dentistry is expected to revolutionize dental care delivery in the future. Dental practices can leverage tele-dentistry to provide virtual consultations, education, and follow-up visits, improving patient engagement and convenience.

3. Patient Data Analytics: Analyzing patient behavior and preferences through patient data analytics can help dental clinics develop individualized engagement strategies. Dental clinics may provide personalized suggestions, forecast patient behavior, and develop specialized communication tactics by evaluating patient data.

4. Patient-Centered Care: A developing trend in the healthcare sector is patient-centered care. Patients anticipate receiving treatment that is customized to their requirements, tastes, and morals. To deliver high-quality care, improve the patient experience, and boost patient involvement, dental offices must implement patient-centered care.

5. Health Literacy: Improving patient health literacy is an essential aspect of patient re-engagement. Health literacy refers to a patient's ability to understand and act upon health information. By improving patient health literacy, dental practices can improve patient engagement, compliance, and health outcomes.

Conclusion:

In conclusion, patient re-engagement is a critical aspect of any successful dental practice. The dental industry is highly competitive and practices must focus on re-engaging with their inactive patients to keep their practice running smoothly. Ignoring patient re-engagement can cost practices a lot of money in lost revenue, as well as negatively affect their online reputation.

It is important to understand the patient journey and analyze patient behavior to identify at-risk patients and develop a segmented re-engagement plan. Practices should utilize personalized follow-up, reminders and notifications, and direct mail to effectively communicate with their inactive patients.

Improving the patient experience is also crucial for patient re-engagement. By focusing on the 4 P's of patient experience, practices can identify opportunities for improvement and create a positive experience for their patients.

Measuring and evaluating re-engagement efforts is important to understand the success of the strategies implemented. Key performance indicators should be tracked to evaluate the effectiveness of re-engagement efforts and refine the strategies if necessary.

Overall, patient re-engagement is an art that requires a thoughtful approach and a combination of strategies to be successful. By implementing the best practices discussed in this book, dental practices can successfully re-engage with their inactive patients and secure a successful future. Looking ahead to the future of patient re-engagement, practices must stay current with technology and continue to innovate to keep up with the ever-changing industry.

CPSIA information can be obtained
at www.ICGtesting.com
Printed in the USA
JSHW072108230523
42147JS00004B/50

9 798890 746894